Empathy by Design
Empathy-Driven Marketing for Libraries

by Sabine Jean Dantus

Association of College and Research Libraries
A division of the American Library Association | Chicago, Illinois 2024

The paper used in this publication meets the minimum requirements of American National Standard for Information Sciences–Permanence of Paper for Printed Library Materials, ANSI Z39.48-1992. ∞

Library of Congress Control Number: 2023952176

Copyright © 2024 by Sabine Jean Dantus

All rights reserved except those which may be granted by Sections 107 and 108 of the Copyright Revision Act of 1976.

Printed in the United States of America.

28 27 26 25 24   5 4 3 2 1

Contents

- vii   **Dedication**
- ix   **Acknowledgments**
- xi   **Preface. Crafting a Foundation for Empowerment and Change: Exploring the Use of Empathy in Library Marketing and DEIA Values**
  - xii   Overview of the Book
  - xiv   Terminology
  - xv   Purpose and Audience
- 1   **Chapter 1. Empathy in Libraries: A New Way to Engage with Your Community**
  - 2   What is Empathy?
  - 4   Empower Your Library's Marketing with Empathy
  - 8   The Process of Empathy in Library Marketing
  - 11   The Takeaway: Empathy in Libraries
- 13   **Chapter 2. Leveraging Compassionate Library Marketing Practices through Empathy and DEIA Values**
  - 15   Empathy as the Foundation of DEIA Practices
  - 17   Empathy and DEIA Practices Lead to Compassionate Actions
  - 18   Cultivating Empathy through Practice
  - 19   Tailor Your Empathic Marketing Approach to DEIA Values
  - 20   Addressing DEIA Values
  - 21   The Takeaway: Bridging the Gap between Libraries and Diverse Audiences
- 23   **Chapter 3. Empathic Design: A Human-centered Solution**
  - 24   Empathic Design Explained
  - 25   Why is Empathic Design Important?
  - 25   Empathic Design in Library Marketing

- 26 Creating Messages That Resonate
- 27 Empathic Design Steps
- 28 Achieving Resource/Program/Service "Nirvana"
- 29 The Takeaway: Empathtic Design in Action
- 30 References

31 Chapter 4. Observation and Identifying the Needs of Users
- 33 Triggers of Use
- 34 Interactions with the User's Environment
- 35 User Customization
- 35 Intangible Attributes of the Library
- 36 Unarticulated User Needs
- 37 Identifying User Motivations
- 38 The Takeaway: Observation and Identification of the Needs of Users
- 39 References

41 Chapter 5. Gathering Accurate, Reliable Data for Informed Decisions
- 44 Let's Talk About Market Research
- 45 How to Begin Your Market Research Journey
- 45 Gathering User Feedback through Surveys, Focus Groups, and Interviews
- 48 Tips for Creating a Survey or Questionnaire
- 50 The Takeaway: Capturing Data and Marketing Research

51 Chapter 6. Uncovering Insights from Data: Reflection and Interpretation
- 52 Examining and Synthesizing Data from Market Research
- 53 Organize the Data into Groups
- 54 Addressing Equity for All Users
- 54 Organizing Data to Address Pain Points
- 55 Conducting a Needs Assessment for Empathic Library Marketing Solutions
- 57 Finding Your Target Audience
- 57 The Takeaway: Reflection and Analysis

59 Chapter 7. Brainstorming or Ideating Solutions
- 60 Brainstorming for Solutions
- 60 Setting up Ground Rules
- 61 Creative Brainstorming Strategies

- 71   The Importance of Brainstorming to Understand the Users' Needs
- 72   The Takeaway: Brainstorming to Develop Solutions

73   Chapter 8. Crafting Empathic Library Marketing Solutions through Prototyping and Testing
- 74   Library Marketing Solutions (Ideas, Tactics, and Strategies)
- 75   The Differences Between Library Marketing Solutions, Channels, Campaigns, Goals, and Strategies
- 76   Comparing a Marketing and an Action Plan: Understanding the Distinctions
- 77   Crafting a Marketing Plan
- 79   Prototyping an Empathy-driven Library Marketing Solution
- 81   Testing the Effectiveness of a Library Marketing Prototype
- 82   Tools and Techniques for Continuous Improvement in Prototyping
- 82   Managing Continuous Improvement in Prototyping
- 83   Strategies for Communicating Library Marketing Prototypes
- 84   The Takeaway: Using the Prototype to Launch Your Library Marketing Solution(s)

85   Chapter 9. The FIRST Values Framework: Putting Empathy into Action or Empathy-Centered Library Marketing Strategies
- 88   Fellow-feeling
- 89   Identification
- 90   Responsiveness
- 91   Self-awareness
- 92   Thoughtfulness
- 93   The Takeaway: The FIRST Values Framework

95   Chapter 10. Evaluating and Measuring Success: Gauging the Impact of Your Library Marketing Strategies
- 96   How to Measure the Success of Your Library Marketing Solutions
- 97   Common Metrics for Measuring Success
- 98   Qualitative Versus Quantitative Evaluation Methods
- 98   Evaluating Library Marketing Effectiveness
- 101   Improving Library Marketing Results
- 103   The Takeaway: Gauging the Impact of Your Library Marketing Strategies

105   Appendix A: Empathic Library Marketing Solutions Toolkit
- 105   Empathic Library Brand
- 106   Conduct Research and Collect Customer Feedback

- 107 Create, Refine, or Revise the Library Mission Statement
- 107 Develop an Empathic Brand Strategy
- 107 Create an Outreach Plan
- 109 Communication Plan
- 113 Empathy-driven Marketing Plan

128 Appendix B: The FIRST Values Framework for Library Marketing Questions

130 Appendix C: Marketing Plan
- 130 Vision
- 130 Core Values
- 131 Executive Summary
- 131 Target Audiences
- 131 Situation Analysis
- 132 Marketing and Outreach Strategies and Tactics (or Objectives)
- 132 Brand Identity
- 133 Key Messages
- 133 Campaign/Action Plan Schedule/Timeline
- 133 Budget
- 133 Communication Samples and Prototypes
- 134 Assessment Results/Reporting/Evaluation/Indicators of Success
- 134 Media List

135 Glossary

143 About the Author

Dedication

I want to dedicate this book, my labor of love, to some of my most treasured and influential people who have enriched my life and physically embody the incredible community by my side.

My mother, Marie Marlene Torchenaud, is someone whose love, selfless devotion, and unwavering support have been invaluable to my life. My husband, Sonny Dantus, has always been a source of love, strength, and support, even during life's most challenging moments. My three sons, Seth, Salem, and Sedrick, each bring unparalleled joy to my life and promise a bright future. My twin sister, Sasha Jean Torchenaud, my lifelong confidante and my siblings Geraldyn, Sandra, Natasha, Sheila, and Ishmael and cousins Dieudonne and Shana were always there for me, providing invaluable support and encouragement throughout my journey. Similarly, my friends Johncy, Alethia, and Dena were always there to provide much-needed encouragement.

Working on this book has been an incredible emotional roller coaster that left me in awe. From the initial flurry of excitement of getting it approved for publication to the anxiety of getting it done to the joy of finishing, the whole process has been a real challenge, especially during the COVID-19 pandemic. But through my ups and downs, I was lucky enough to have some fantastic allies by my side, believing in what was possible even when doubt crept into my mind. Knowing that others believed in me gave me the confidence and motivation to complete this book that never faltered. Your presence allowed me to continue even when the road seemed too challenging.

I want to express my utmost gratitude to all those I haven't mentioned by name, like the Dantus, St. Germain, Jean, Philogene, Noelette, and Felix families and friends not mentioned individually but who have supported me. You have been there for me through the best and most difficult times, and I'm genuinely grateful for that. From the bottom of my heart, thank you for being a part of my journey. Without the support and belief of these wonderful people God has placed in my life, this book would not have been possible.

Acknowledgments

This recognition is a testament to the hard work and dedication that went into writing and publishing this book. I am deeply grateful to the Association of College and Research Libraries (ACRL) Publishing for taking a chance on a book on library marketing and empathy. I thank Erin Nevius and the advisory board for taking a chance on a book about empathy and marketing for libraries. I am grateful for their support in making this book possible. Thank you to ACRL for all you do to help academic and research librarians and library workers. You are a strong voice for our profession nationally and internationally through the American Library Association (ALA). Thank you for all that you do! I am proud to be a member of ALA, RUSA, and ACRL, and I stand with you in supporting our vital role in higher education and libraries.

I want to thank my former colleagues at the Eugene M. and Christine E. Lynn University Library, Stacy Alesi, Leecy Barnett, Tsukasa Cherkaoui, Jordan Chussler, Lea Iadarola, Robert Leigh, Jared Wellman, for their immense support during my time there. In particular, I would like to thank Amy Filiatreau, library director, for her guidance and patience. Amy was a constant source of support, and I am grateful to have had the opportunity to work with her. I would also like to thank my fellow students and part-time marketing team members at Lynn University for their hard work and dedication: Wanda Francois, Christelle Mehu, Gardith Desauguste, Nino Ruiz, Lensa Jeudy, and Angela Destine. I am proud to have led and worked with such a talented and driven marketing and outreach team. I want to thank all of the faculty and staff at Lynn University who have supported me throughout my time there, especially Harika Rao, Antonella Regueiro, Stefanie Powers, Cesar Santalo, Martin Phillips, David Jaffe, Dawn Dubriel, Robert P. Watson, Baraka Packer, and Sindee Kerker, to name a few. Working with all of you has been a privilege, and I am still genuinely grateful to have known you all.

Thank you to the Florida International University (FIU) Libraries administration for allowing me to keep working on my outreach and marketing plans and ideas. In particular, I would like to thank my chair, Gricel Dominguez, for her willingness to give me the time and space to write. Without her encouragement, I would not have been able to finish this book. Also, thanks to the rest of the faculty and staff at FIU Libraries for their assistance and support, especially Kittiphong Suwanmanneedang; I appreciate everything you have done in the past (as a student worker) and present (as an FIU alumnus returning as a librarian).

PREFACE

Crafting a Foundation for Empowerment and Change:

Exploring the Use of Empathy in Library Marketing and DEIA Values

The library is a universal resource where knowledge and information meet. However, over the years, these public spaces have been subjected to certain expectations and practices that no longer serve the advancement of equal access in positive ways. In light of the recent global pandemic, wars, and racial issues, libraries must develop strategies, campaigns, and messages that show they care about the lives of their diverse communities. I must admit that writing this book was challenging but rewarding because I wanted to make sure that library marketers would not only understand the importance of using empathy in marketing but also as a tool for advancing our profession's values for diversity, equity, inclusion, and access (DEIA). The strategies outlined in this book can help bridge the gap between tradition and modernity by giving you the tools to make your marketing more targeted and empathic.

With this open, empathic dialogue of mutual respect, I hope libraries will become safe places for users of all backgrounds to learn, think, and discover. Empathy is an essential skill for people working in libraries, and this book will help my colleagues develop and improve their skills in empathic marketing. Also,

I hope *Empathy by Design* will help people in libraries learn more about empathy and inspire them to do more research on the subject. Empathy has been crucial to my work as a library marketer. Even though each audience I've spoken to has been different, my ability to understand others has helped me explain our mission and vision to many different groups. Because I empathize with other people, I can understand their backgrounds and points of view. Understanding the users lets me be creative and realistic in crafting my messages and ensure they reach users meaningfully. Empathy allows me to take pride in sharing our library's successes and being involved in communities that help advance our mission. Researching empathy-based practices in library marketing has opened my eyes to how empathy can help us better understand our patrons' needs and create an inclusive environment.

As a strategist, I believe that when it comes to marketing libraries, an empathy-based approach is essential to ensure that all library resources are seen as relevant and accessible. My experience in creating empathetic strategies goes beyond superficial idealism; it involves recognizing that different people can be impacted differently by messages and campaigns and designing solutions to account for this. When empathy-driven initiatives are at the core of my strategies, it ensures that all aspects of library marketing efforts are thought through. It is also critical for comprehending and connecting with various audiences, which can help create a more inviting atmosphere. With empathy as the basis of our collective endeavors, I am confident that we can come together to support and promote the positive works of libraries.

Also, empathy is a crucial tool for libraries as we work to bridge divides in a society that is often quick to judge and mischaracterize people from different cultures, communities, or identity groups. Empathy can assist libraries in expanding their mission from simply providing services to actively embracing a wide variety of people and inspiring them to engage more with the library's resources. Empathy becomes a significant factor in crafting a successful marketing strategy by understanding that each library user has different needs, curiosities, backgrounds, and reasons for visiting the library. Compassionate libraries can create more positive experiences for their patrons, develop more effective marketing strategies, and create a sense of belonging and community. I aim to give libraries the tools they need to break down barriers and foster empathic marketing strategies that reach all users.

Overview of the Book

Empathy by Design: Empathy-driven Marketing for Libraries is motivated by empathy for libraries and users. I aim to give you (the reader) a deeper understanding of empathy as a tool so that your library can make empathic, meaningful, and long-lasting changes to your marketing efforts. *Empathy by Design* is an empathic approach to marketing that focuses on understanding and appreciating what library users and visitors genuinely desire. To successfully market libraries, it's essential to recognize the nuances of how people think and feel about libraries. *Empathy by Design* uses various research techniques, such as qualitative interviews and focus groups, to gain insight into user needs and preferences. This information can then create tailored campaigns that meet user expectations.

This type of marketing strategy goes beyond simply providing users with resource information or programs; it seeks to understand the motivations behind why people visit the library in the first place. By taking an empathetic approach, marketing for libraries can be much more effective because it allows for personalization that resonates with users on a deeper level. *Empathy by Design* also considers various demographics, such as age, gender, socioeconomic status, and educational background, when developing library marketing campaigns. This ensures that campaigns are designed with all types of library users in mind, so they are relevant to everyone's individual needs. Additionally, this method allows for the segmentation of messages to be tailored specifically toward different groups within the population.

Librarians can craft successful messages by understanding their audience's wants and needs. Furthermore, this type of marketing considers any potential barriers (such as price points or technological requirements) that may exist so solutions can be created to ensure everyone has access to library resources regardless of these constraints. Overall, *Empathy by Design* presents ways to better connect with patrons and maximize a library's outreach efforts while meeting the unique needs of every library visitor—no matter their background or motivation for using the library's services. With empathy, librarians can better understand current issues from an intersectional perspective and learn more about the diverse users in their community. My goal is for you to understand empathy in marketing so well that you can make informed decisions that lead to more impactful marketing and outreach plans.

Empathy by Design also explores how empathy helps us recognize the nuances within our communities that often go unnoticed without careful consideration. In doing so, we create experiences for patrons that meet their needs and respect their unique backgrounds and experiences. By recognizing and valuing this diversity of perspectives within our communities, libraries can gain valuable insights into which services are desired by each group they serve. With a clear understanding of what drives people's decisions and behaviors, libraries can craft marketing campaigns that move beyond simply getting consumers' attention—they can start motivating them to act or engage further with relevant offerings provided by the library. Equipped with this knowledge, library professionals can create messages explicitly designed for different groups within their community and ensure different types of users feel seen and heard meaningfully.

The chapters in this book provide step-by-step instructions on strategically using empathy and empathic design in library marketing. It offers real-world solutions on how libraries can better understand their target audience through empathy. Additionally, you will learn how to develop messages that foster meaningful connections with your audiences and inspire engagement from library professionals, users, and potential users.

Rather than responding reactively, empathy-driven marketing techniques can help library professionals proactively step into the shoes of their users to gain insight into and understand their points of view. This approach to library marketing allows for more effective, efficient campaigns that ultimately lead to greater customer satisfaction across all demographics.

Empathy by Design is an incredibly valuable source of information for libraries seeking equitable results for their entire user base—helping them foster greater customer satisfaction and loyalty. Utilizing principles associated with empathic design also helps you identify groups of potential users who may have been previously overlooked.

Also included is advice on analyzing user feedback as part of an ongoing evaluation process so that you can further refine existing strategies or develop new ones based on data-backed insights. Lastly, I discuss methods for integrating user data into other aspects of library operations, such as staffing decisions, resource allocation, and event planning, to ensure that library activities remain tailored to the needs of patrons.

Terminology

Instead of referring to librarians as the only people to market libraries, I address you, the reader, as a library marketer. This book uses the terms "users," "customers," "patrons," and "target audience" interchangeably. All four terms refer to library users, including students, staff, faculty, administrators, and community members. When I refer to people who use the library as "users," the term "users" is intended only in this book's context; that term should not be used in your marketing materials. It's much more polite to refer to your users as "students," "parents," "alumni," "faculty," "staff," "community members," etc. in your marketing materials, which can then help you divide the market into different groups (market segmentation). In the context of libraries, the word "product" can be interchangeably referred to as a "program," "resource," or "service." In *Empathy by Design*, "solutions" are also used to describe marketing campaigns, promotions, and materials. If you encounter a term, you do not understand while reading this book, please consult the glossary at the end of the book for clarification.

Purpose and Audience

This book is directed primarily toward directors, deans, librarians, library professionals, and marketing specialists in academic libraries. However, this guide is geared toward librarians, professionals, and marketers, including those who want to make the user experience more inclusive and equitable. As we discuss empathic design as a vehicle for library marketing, we will review what empathy means and how it can be effectively employed. Empathy is a key factor in the success of libraries; it requires understanding the users' needs and having an appreciation for their unique perspectives. To that end, this book focuses on helping library professionals understand and implement empathic design principles. The ideal reader for this book would be a person who chairs or participates in an outreach committee or working group or for those working solo marketing services in their libraries. The audience will benefit from a more in-depth analysis of how to effectively reach their target communities, understanding the importance of behind-the-scenes planning and implementation, and the ultimate goal of increasing library usage.

Marketing initiatives require a comprehensive approach that involves understanding the needs and wants of your target audience, identifying opportunities to engage, and creating tailored messages that resonate with them. It's also important to consider which communication channels are most effective for reaching different segments within your community and how best to track progress. Successful outreach initiatives should be designed with both short-term and long-term goals, guaranteeing your message reaches your users and resulting in greater awareness of library offerings today and in the future. Marketers who are responsible for outreach within libraries must think holistically about the process from start to finish, developing an action plan that focuses on gathering data and feedback from users, setting measurable goals based on those insights, creating meaningful content that resonates with their community members, then tracking results over time to make needed adjustments. As part of this plan, evaluating existing programs for effectiveness and identifying gaps where more targeted efforts may be required is also important. Additionally, establishing partnerships and pursuing creative collaborations outside of the library can help extend reach even further.

Overall, there are many moving parts to successful outreach initiatives within libraries; however, thoughtful strategy and creativity can achieve these objectives! By taking a holistic approach to outreach efforts—including careful planning, ongoing evaluation, and creative execution—libraries can provide meaningful content that resonates with their audiences while seeing tangible results over time. This book will help library professionals use empathic design principles to create marketing plans tailored to library users' interests and needs effectively.

References

Shontz, M. L., Parker, J. C., & Parker, R. (2004). What do librarians think about marketing? A survey of public librarians' attitudes toward the marketing of library services. *The Library Quarterly, 74*, no. 1, 63–84.

CHAPTER 1

Empathy in Libraries:
A New Way to Engage with Your Community

"Empathy drives connection, and sympathy fuels disconnection."
– Brené Brown

Libraries have always been places of learning and knowledge. In today's society, libraries are also places of empathy. Libraries are essential in creating a secure and inclusive space that caters to all community members, offering resources, services, and learning opportunities. By fostering a welcoming and friendly atmosphere, libraries provide a haven for people of diverse backgrounds, interests, and needs. Their commitment to facilitating access to information, resources, and services ensures everyone feels supported and valued. Indeed, libraries are vital to any community, promoting education, lifelong learning, and social cohesion. Many individuals may still hold the view that libraries are outdated and unnecessary. However, with effective marketing, it is possible to shift this perception by understanding library users and their needs through empathy. As a result, you can help change the public's perception of what libraries are and what they do, leading to more funding and support for libraries.

An integral part of a library's mission is to provide a safe and welcoming space for individuals of all backgrounds. Libraries have the unique opportunity to offer free access to books, materials, programs, services, and events that can help people learn new skills or gain knowledge in areas they are passionate about. From offering job training workshops or computer classes so patrons may be better equipped for success in their careers to hosting book clubs or story times where children and adults alike can come together as one community, empathy lies at the heart of a library's dedication to providing support no matter what an individual's background might be. With empathy, libraries can tap into the needs and desires of their patrons, leading to personalized experiences that reflect the priorities and creativity of their communities. This same empathy can also be used in library marketing efforts, allowing libraries to show a human touch and create an emotional connection with users, forming a foundation for loyalty. Most importantly, empathy allows us to connect on an individual level with users, encouraging open dialogue and building trust between the library and its users—all essential prerequisites for creating an engaged user base of brand ambassadors who will help spread the word about your library.

Libraries must go beyond their traditional roles and meet the changing demands of a growing, more diverse user base. To do so, they require an in-depth understanding of how potential library users view electronic resources compared to books or other physical items. Libraries must equip themselves with innovative marketing strategies and cater specifically to individual demographic groups that don't typically rely on them for service— this is more key than ever. It is important for librarians to proactively learn about the needs of their diverse patrons and ensure that they provide the necessary resources and services to meet those needs. I believe understanding patrons can be solved through empathy in library marketing.

What is Empathy?

Empathy, as Miller and Wallis (2011) state, is "the ability to understand and share the feelings of others" (p. 122). This could mean a person or group of people. Empathy is a central concept in psychology, philosophy, and the humanistic and social sciences. It is also an essential part of interpersonal relationships. Empathy is often called a "soft skill" because it involves understanding and getting along with other people. Empathy can be developed through education, experience, and practice.

The first step in using empathy as a marketing tool is understanding what it is and how it works. Empathy can be understood as a way of looking at the world through the eyes of others—being able to understand their feelings and perspectives. Empathy aims to put us in someone else's shoes and imagine what it would be like for them. Empathy isn't just about being nice or trying to please everyone; it's also about being honest and transparent in your communications so that users can trust you and your library. It has been demonstrated that empathy strengthens relationships by facilitating mutual understanding. Miller and

Wallis (2011) remind us that empathy helps build relationships with users. It allows us to connect with people on their level, develop trust, and aid in developing rapport with them (Miller & Wallis, 2011).

Klare, Behney, and Kenney (2014) point out that libraries are places where personal connections should be valued above all else. Klare, Behney, and Kenney (2014) put forth a compelling argument for the importance of empathy in library marketing: "Feel first, think second" (p. 1). In other words, library marketers should try to solve users' problems only after they have listened to them. This motto is based on the idea that it is often more important to be seen and heard and that doing so might solve the problem. Providing this understanding helps to make the users feel valued and listened to, creating strong connections with the library that can extend far beyond the scope of any particular query or concern.

One of the most essential things a librarian can do to establish strong relationships with users is to put the user first rather than jumping in with their opinions and solutions. For the library to be successful in its marketing efforts, it should listen to and empathize with its users. This "feel first, think second" philosophy enables library marketers to truly comprehend what customers need right down to the core of the problem identified. Libraries can foster loyalty among their users and improve the services they can offer them in the future by investing a little more time and effort in creating that personal connection with them. Even as technology advances and more digital resources become available, libraries will remain where human connection is most important.

When you act with empathy, you can build stronger relationships, better help your users, and create an atmosphere of mutual respect, trust, and understanding. To truly empathize with your library users, you need to understand how they are feeling and the experiences that have caused those feelings.

Empathy matters in marketing libraries because it allows us to be more creative in our approaches to library users. It can be the cornerstone of effective library marketing. With compassion as the primary focus of our marketing efforts, libraries can move away from traditional marketing tactics and instead focus on providing experiences tailored to our communities. Through this approach, libraries can build trust with their patrons and foster a sense of belonging, which is essential for developing a solid library culture. Not only will empathy provide library users with a feeling of welcome, respect, and understanding, but it can also help library professionals better understand varying user needs so they can serve them more effectively.

Developing empathy is essential to continuous improvement, enabling us to cultivate a deeper understanding and respect for other personalities, cultures, and situations. Through this practice, we can become more effective and understanding in our communications with library users. One way to be more empathetic is to listen without judging or feeling the need to give advice. It's important to have conversations to share our thoughts and learn about what the other person is going through. Also, accepting feedback and learning from mistakes are great ways to help ourselves and others become more empathetic. Empathy flourishes when we are prepared to be vulnerable in our connections with one another and accountable for trying to understand alternative points of view.

Empower Your Library's Marketing with Empathy

Marketing creates and delivers messages promoting a resource, program, or service. This means determining what your target audience wants and needs and making content and campaigns that communicate how the library meets those needs. Empathy can be a powerful tool for creating compelling and engaging marketing solutions that meet the needs of library users and give them something of value through library services and resources. Empathy can help libraries understand their users' needs and pain points, develop new ideas, make prototypes, use design thinking, test and iterate solutions, and measure how well their marketing strategies are working.

Empathy in library marketing becomes more than just a feeling; it becomes a valid, constructive, and valuable tool in library marketing. Empathy is a core value and is not sympathy for your users. Empathy goes beyond sympathy—simply feeling bad for someone else's situation—by enabling us to see the world through another person's eyes and better recognize our users' pain points. Libraries are more than just repositories of information; they are sanctuaries of empathy. Despite the ever-evolving technological landscape, libraries remain a vital source of connection and community for people everywhere. Libraries that market with empathy prioritize human connection and offer a sense of community that an algorithm or artificial intelligence can't replicate. Libraries give people from any walk of life a safe place to read without judgment, discuss common interests, and share perspectives. Despite global changes in how we search for facts and digest the news, libraries remain an outpost of empathy and intellectual freedom where we can connect and be inspired.

Libraries serve a wide variety of users, from students to researchers to members of the general public. While there is no such thing as a specific target user, libraries can tailor their services and collections to meet the needs of their communities. For example, a school library will focus on providing resources that support the curriculum, while a public library will offer a more diverse range of materials. When you view your marketing through empathy, you can create content, design campaigns, and make decisions that appeal to your audience and help you connect with them on a deeper level.

Empathy is a previewer for libraries. Empathy helps the staff figure out what the public will need and choose resources ahead of time to meet those needs. Empathy allows library professionals to get closer to the public and build relationships based on trust, acceptance, and mutual respect, fostering a sense of belonging that encourages people to return to the library. In summary, empathy is now required in libraries if you want to draw and hold on to patrons over time.

Empathy must play a significant role in contemporary library marketing, allowing the library to connect with its members meaningfully and give them access to resources that will help them grow personally and professionally. So, it shouldn't be surprising that more and more libraries include this idea in their mission statements. Here are some examples of how to use empathy in your marketing strategies:

- **Personalization.** Personalization is the key to effective marketing. By understanding your customers and what they need, you can create personalized experiences that will make them feel valued and appreciated.
- **Customer service.** Providing excellent customer service is essential for building customer trust and loyalty. Providing timely and helpful responses to customer inquiries demonstrates that you care about their needs and appreciate their business.
- **Listen.** Listening to your customers is a great way to demonstrate empathy. Taking the time to understand what they're saying and responding with genuine interest helps build trust.
- **Show appreciation.** Showing your users that you appreciate their business is a great way to demonstrate empathy. A simple "thank you" or a special offer can go a long way in showing your appreciation.
- **Storytelling.** Storytelling is a powerful tool to connect with your customers. Creating stories that resonate with your customers can create an emotional connection to help you stand out.

With the right approach, marketing with empathy can help boost engagement, loyalty, and revenue. When you know what your users want, why they want it, and what drives them, you can make library marketing plans, campaigns, content, channels, and tactics more likely to connect with your community and meet their needs with solutions tailored to them.

Empathy in library marketing requires two key things: make it personal and be transparent. For example, if you're marketing a new resource to library users, it's essential to be clear about the service and how it works. If you are upfront and honest about the service and why you think it is valuable, users are more likely to be receptive and even excited about trying it out. Your audiences are more likely to respond if you speak to them personally. Address their needs through your marketing materials and campaigns and show you understand what they're looking for in a library. In terms of transparency, tell your audience what your library offers and be upfront about any limitations. Trust is built through transparency.

Many libraries may take a "one-size-fits-all" approach to marketing, but this is ineffective if you want to reach potential new customers. Knowing your current and potential patrons' demographics, interests, and lifestyles can help you craft targeted messages that resonate with those audiences. For example, suppose your library has traditionally served seniors or retirees. In that case, you may want to focus on how the library can help them stay connected with their communities or keep up with technology trends. On the other hand, if you are trying to reach younger patrons, such as students or young professionals, you could focus on how the library can be a resource for research projects and career development. By understanding who your audience is and what they need from the library, you can create content that speaks directly to those needs.

When you understand the needs of your audience and provide solutions that meet those needs through valuable content or engaging programming, people will be more likely to come back, leading to better patron loyalty over time. In this way, empathy is essential for any library looking to survive in today's competitive market. When you provide what users want, you create a loyal connection beyond simply checking out books or using the computers. Instead, users feel part of something larger that meets their intellectual and emotional needs. And that is what will make your library stand out in today's competitive landscape.

When we take the time to empathize with our users, they are more likely to provide us with the information we need to serve their library needs better. In 2004, Shontz, Parker, and Parker released a study that suggested physical libraries would become less important as people met less often in them. Fast forward to today, and that sentiment has unfortunately not changed. The COVID-19 pandemic has only exacerbated this shift, presenting the challenge of adapting library marketing techniques to operate in an increasingly digital world so that library users can still feel connected to the service despite using it from home or virtually. While this change has brought challenges, it can also allow us to reach new audiences and offer more innovative services.

Once empathy is woven into what you do in your library, empathy "allows you to work in a wide variety of spheres of influence" (Klare, Behney, and Kenney 2014, p. 22). As Miller and Wallis (2011) remind us, empathy is the key to successful interactions, and they describe empathy as the secret sauce of "a successful information transaction" (Miller and Wallis, 2011, p. 122). Empathy is an innate ability. Psychologists note that some people are born with it more than others, but anyone can better empathize with practice (Miller 2019).

To provide services and programs that are genuinely empathetic, it is essential to understand the meaning of empathy and how it can be applied in practice. Theresa Wiseman, a nursing scholar and clinical professor from the UK, explains that the "Four Elements of Empathy" are seeing the world through another person's eyes, appreciating them as people, understanding how they feel, and then letting them know that you understand (see Figure 1). The ability to put oneself in another person's shoes and respond appropriately is at the heart of empathy. If you take the time to learn about your users, you can create resources and services that are more likely to provide them with a positive experience.

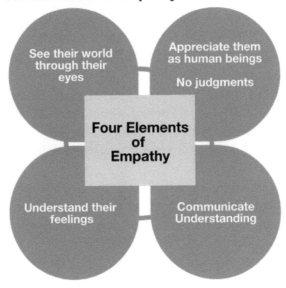

Figure 1. Theresa Wiseman's "Four Elements of Empathy" can help you understand the meaning of empathy and how it can be applied in practice.

Spending time thinking about how our users see the world helps us better understand and meet their unique needs. Making assumptions about what users want or need is easy without empathy, leading to resources and services that fall short of user expectations.

The Process of Empathy in Library Marketing

Empathy is a powerful marketing tool that can help you connect with your users and show them how your service can benefit them. You can start using empathy in your marketing today by understanding what it is and how it works. Empathy is not just a feeling but a process. You engage in empathy when you think about the user and the user's context. However, it is not enough to think about the user. We all do that, right? Acting based on these thoughts makes this process different and more impactful. When you think about your users, what do you do? You probably try to put yourself in their shoes and imagine what their life is like, what their problems are, and what their goals are. When you use empathy in library marketing, you consider how potential users might feel if they used your services. You must then show users the benefits of your service instead of just listing them in a brochure.

Here are a few ways that libraries can use empathy in their marketing efforts:

- Understand what pain points or needs your users are trying to address with your services.
- Consider what emotions your services evoke in people. Are they making them feel excited, educated, or entertained?
- Use language that is relatable and understandable to your users.
- Focus on your target audience's needs and wants rather than what you want to sell them.
- Share stories and experiences that your users can relate to, which can help you connect with them emotionally.
- Build trust with your target audience by being transparent and honest about your intentions.

Empathy can help librarians identify the best ways to engage their users and effectively promote their services through meticulous research, targeted outreach, thoughtful content creation, personalizing campaigns for different user groups, connecting with stakeholders on a human level, empathy-based customer service tactics, and more. Here are a few examples of successful library marketing ideas or campaigns based on empathy:

- Create a customized, interactive "story time" page with content tailored to different ages and interests.
- Offer virtual learn-at-home events highlighting resources that can benefit those who are homebound.
- Invite library users to collaborate in creating a short list of essential books or periodicals around different topics.
- Offer an online patron survey to gain insight into the needs and concerns of your target audience.

Such empathy-based campaigns can help a library build stronger relationships within its community and foster a sense of belonging among its members. This, in turn, leads to increased engagement with the library's resources, which helps create a more vibrant learning environment for everyone involved. When the library prioritizes the needs of its patrons, they feel a sense of belonging and connection. This fosters a positive environment that encourages individuals to return and continue to engage with the library.

If you're stuck in a rut with your library marketing and not seeing the conversions you want, it might be time to try the empathy approach. What are your user's needs? What are their pain points? What are their expectations and goals regarding their use of the library? How can your service fulfill these needs? Asking these questions and paying close attention to the answers is the best way to create marketing campaigns that connect with users.

For example, if you find out that parents are concerned about the research needs of their children, as students, you could create a series of blog posts or social media posts about how the library can help with projects and papers. By tracking the number of people who visit your library and what you have spent on library services, you can better understand which marketing campaigns are working and which ones need improvement. Every touchpoint should be an opportunity to connect with users on a deeper level and understand their needs and desires.

The consistency of your marketing campaigns and your library's mission reinforces its commitment to its core values and purpose. It helps to establish trust and credibility while demonstrating a genuine commitment to meeting the needs and aspirations of the community. Your marketing should reflect the core values and mission of the library, and your campaigns should directly support and reinforce the goals and purpose of the library. Here are a few key points to consider for mission alignment:

- When promoting your library's services, programs, and resources, it's essential to communicate, tailor your messaging, maintain consistent branding, use storytelling, provide educational content, encourage community engagement, regularly review your marketing materials, collaborate with stakeholders, and measure and gather feedback.
- To achieve clear communication, ensure your messaging is transparent, straightforward, and aligned with your library's mission. This will help patrons understand the library's purpose and how it benefits the community.
- For targeted messaging, tailor your marketing messages to specific segments of your community while still keeping your mission in

focus. For instance, if your mission involves promoting literacy, target messages to parents, educators, and readers with programs and resources that support this goal.
- Consistent branding is essential to reinforce your library's identity and purpose. Ensure your branding elements, such as logos, colors, and slogans, align with your library's mission and values.
- Use storytelling in your marketing campaigns to illustrate how the library's mission positively impacts the lives of community members. Share success stories and testimonials highlighting the library's role in fulfilling its mission.
- Provide educational content that aligns with your library's mission. Create informative materials, workshops, or webinars that help patrons better understand the library's purpose and how they can benefit from its services.
- Encourage community members to actively participate in and contribute to the library's mission. This can be through volunteer opportunities, feedback, or collaborative initiatives that align with your library's goals.
- Regularly review your marketing materials and campaigns to ensure they align with your mission. As your library's mission evolves, update your messaging accordingly.
- Work closely with staff, trustees, and community members to ensure marketing messages accurately reflect the library's mission. Input from those who are deeply connected to the library can help refine your campaigns.
- Continuously monitor the effectiveness of your marketing efforts and gather feedback from the community. This data can help you adjust your messaging to reflect better your mission and the changing needs of your patrons.

The Takeaway: Empathy in Libraries

Users often want to know they can use your service to achieve their goals and improve their lives. For example, if a library markets itself as a place for research and study, it can target ads at students struggling with papers or exams and explain how the library can improve their research. In this way, marketing becomes about selling a resource, program, or service and helping people understand how that resource or service can benefit them. If you can show them this, you'll be on your way to marketing with empathy—understanding your users' needs and designing solutions that meet them.

The importance of considering unspoken user needs must be considered. Empathy is not just a feeling but a process that includes trying to see the world from another person's perspective, understanding their inner state and feelings, and then taking action to create solutions that meet the user's needs.

Empathy builds relationships by creating marketing content that resonates with your users. This might include blog posts, social media posts, or videos. Be sure to make sure your messaging and branding are consistent across all channels. Before you move on to Chapter 2, let's make sure you have a good understanding of the goals of empathy in library marketing:

- Understand your users' feelings.
- Gain a good understanding of your users' needs.
- Design solutions that meet those needs.
- Make sure your messaging is consistent with your mission.

References

Klare, D., Behney, M., & Kenney, B. F. (2014). Emotional intelligence in a stupid world. *Library Hi Tech News*.

Leonard, D., & Rayport, J. F. (1997). Spark innovation through empathic design. *Harvard Business Review*, 75 (1997): 102–115.

Miller, F., & Wallis, J. (2011). Social interaction and the role of empathy in information and knowledge management: A literature review. Journal of Education for Library and Information Science, 122–132.

Miller, C. C. (2019). How to be more empathetic. The New York Times.

Shontz, M. L., Parker, J. C., & Parker, R. (2004). What do librarians think about marketing? A survey of public librarians' attitudes toward the marketing of library services. The Library Quarterly, 74, no. 1 (2004): 63–84.

Wiseman, T. (1996). A concept analysis of empathy. Journal of Advanced Nursing, 23, no. 6, 1162–1167.

CHAPTER 2

Leveraging Compassionate Library Marketing Practices through Empathy and DEIA Values

"It is not our differences that divide us. It is our inability to recognize, accept, and celebrate those differences." – Audre Lorde

Diversity is at the heart of what makes human beings thrive as a culture. Working toward equity means understanding that everyone needs to be treated equally and given the same opportunities. In today's world, diversity, equity, inclusion, and accessibility (DEIA) are important values many organizations strive to achieve. DEIA is an essential value for libraries and librarians. Libraries are a cornerstone of society and culture, providing access to information, education, entertainment, and enlightenment. As such, libraries should strive to exemplify the values of empathy, diversity, equity, inclusion, and accessibility. These values are essential for building trust with library patrons and creating compassionate marketing practices. But it takes more than just DEIA values alone to create a truly compassionate environment—it requires empathy and practices that center on DEIA values.

Empathy + Diversity, Equity, Inclusion, and Accessibility Values = Compassionate Practices in Library Marketing

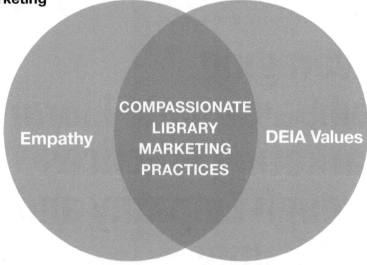

Figure 2. Venn's diagram shows where empathy and the values of diversity, equity, inclusion, and accessibility have commonality.

Empathy is critical to understanding the systemic problems faced by Black, Indigenous, and People of Color (BIPOC) as well as those facing LGBTQ people, women, and people with disabilities. While those in positions of power may not recognize or acknowledge these obstacles from a place of privilege and authority, being aware of the nuances that shape oppression can help us unlock why specific populations are disproportionately affected by prejudice and discrimination. Empathy is a significant core value to cultivate to gain a deeper understanding of historical injustices while recognizing our responsibilities in the fight for a more just and equitable future. It is important to remember that everyone has unique experiences that inform their perspectives.

Therefore, it is necessary to take the time to understand those perspectives when crafting marketing messages. Taking a few extra moments to consider how messages could be perceived can go a long way toward connecting with your patrons on an emotional level. When those in positions of authority or power carry lopsided perspectives on systemic oppression of minority populations, they might not comprehend the magnitude of injustice at play. Demonstrating an awareness of these issues in your library marketing initiatives—or any other place—involves cultivating an understanding of power dynamics and privilege, which requires empathy.

Library marketing is a powerful tool to fight discrimination and exclusion, and librarians can be leaders in ensuring the services they provide are accessible to all. Recognizing that people are unique and developing strategies for marketing and outreach based on DEIA means practicing inclusion for all users, regardless of their backgrounds or abilities. By taking steps such as implementing diversity training, developing inclusive policies, increasing accessibility features, and promoting empathy among staff members, libraries can create an environment that welcomes everyone equally into their establishments. Ultimately, this will improve service delivery, benefiting users and staff alike.

By showing genuine empathy and understanding in your library marketing practices, you can create an inclusive environment where gender identity, LGBTQ identities, individuals who are differently abled, and other excluded or marginalized populations feel respected. By focusing on creativity with library promotions and platforms that feature genuine representation, library marketers can strive to make those formerly excluded or marginalized populations more visible within the library. When library marketers demonstrate an understanding of various groups' experiences in their library marketing plans, this can help reassure library users that library professionals care about creating an inclusive library environment for everyone.

Additionally, library professionals can leverage library marketing practices by demonstrating empathy with activist campaigns and initiatives and allocating resources to organizations addressing equity and access-related issues. Together, this shows a commitment to making the library an equitable place where no reader is left behind. Understanding what each person needs within the context of DEIA initiatives facilitates more profound connections with communities and allows librarians to develop meaningful strategies that empower those communities. Without such a sharpened focus on inclusion and advocacy through empathy, marketing efforts may fail to address disparities between groups adequately.

Empathy as the Foundation of DEIA Practices

Empathy allows staff members to look beyond the surface level and understand how systems of oppression may be impacting users' access to services or resources. This is essential when creating effective DEIA practices that foster understanding and respect within library settings. Libraries are more than just places where books are stored; they are community hubs that offer access to knowledge and resources for all. The four DEIA components—diversity, equity, inclusion, and accessibility—uphold the core values of compassionate and empathetic library marketing work and create a welcoming environment for everyone.

Diversity refers to the variety of characteristics that make individuals unique. Promoting diverse voices means actively seeking out underrepresented authors, speakers, and other content creators who can provide meaningful insights into different perspectives and experiences. This helps foster an environment of understanding and creates an inclusive atmosphere.

Equity means ensuring everyone has access to the same resources, regardless of their background, race, gender identity, sexuality, or any other factor that could lead to inequitable treatment within the library; it's about fairness and justice. It means providing access to materials for people with disabilities or making sure that individuals from different socioeconomic backgrounds have access to relevant materials and services at no additional cost. For example, if one group receives preferential treatment over another due to their race or gender identity, then there is an apparent lack of equity present within the system.

Inclusion means recognizing everyone's right to participate. Inclusion goes hand in hand with equity; it focuses on creating an environment where everyone feels welcomed regardless of their differences. This includes offering programs explicitly tailored for diverse populations such as special needs children or members of the LGBTQ+ community.

Accessibility means making sure services are available for all people, regardless of ability or physical or mental impairment. This includes making sure that library websites are user-friendly for those users who are visually or hearing impaired by using alt text descriptions for images on webpages and providing transcripts for video content. It also includes offering assistive technology such as large print books or audiobooks for users who may be unable to read standard-size print materials due to vision impairments. These measures help ensure that all library users can access materials without barriers or difficulties, regardless of their ability level or disability. Lastly, accessibility ensures that everyone has the same amount of access to physical space and digital platforms like websites and databases. Making sure all materials are available online helps those with disabilities who may not be able to visit physical locations due to physical limitations. Also, libraries must ensure their physical spaces are accessible to everyone.

Together with empathy, these values emphasize the importance of being open-minded when communicating with library patrons and understanding how different backgrounds can shape one's experiences. This can create a powerful connection between patrons and libraries, which will ultimately help drive foot traffic into the physical space as well as online engagement with library digital services.

Empathy and DEIA Practices Lead to Compassionate Actions

Compassionate practices are essential for any public institution, but especially for libraries, which strive to provide equal access for everyone regardless of race, gender identity, or other characteristics that might make them feel excluded from accessing library services. By infusing empathy into library practices and incorporating DEIA principles into existing policies, such as collection development policies and hiring processes, libraries can begin down the path toward making sure none of its users feel unwelcome or excluded from accessing the wealth of knowledge stored within its walls.

Compassionate practices involve acting with kindness and understanding toward others. This includes speaking up when we witness unfairness or injustice, making sure our spaces are inclusive for everyone who visits them, using our privilege for good rather than exploiting it, etc. These actions not only benefit those around us but also help us grow as individuals by giving us a better understanding of different people's lives and perspectives.

Compassionate practices create a safe space for everyone involved, allowing people from all backgrounds to feel respected and valued for their opinions without fear of judgment or exclusion. It also encourages open dialogue within an organization by reinforcing trust between its members, which leads to greater collaboration across teams and departments. Empathy combined with DEIA practices leads to compassionate actions that benefit everyone involved in any situation or organization. When we prioritize empathy over anything else, we build trust with those around us, which creates an open dialogue necessary for collaboration among teams or departments; this ultimately leads to more efficient problem-solving where everyone benefits equally from the results.

Once a library has assessed its DEIA practices, it can start making new policies and procedures or improve the ones it already has. In the following few chapters, you'll learn about strategies that can help you create marketing initiatives based on empathy and empathic design. This will help you make decisions as a library marketer, working from a place of equity and inclusion to best meet the needs of their many users. It also requires us to be aware of our own possible biases and be able to spot them when we talk to our users or try to sell them something.

The most beneficial action we can take for anyone who enters one of our libraries is to work toward making them feel as welcome as is humanly possible.

Empathy can help you learn more about your users and their needs, allowing the library to provide better information, resources, and user programs. You will have achieved true DEIA values when your library can treat its users fairly and honestly without any hidden agendas or biases. When combined with empathy, this results in acting as a catalyst for developing compassionate actions.

We must develop initiatives that show empathy for many different experiences and points of view because some groups may need extra care. For example, students from other countries may need help overcoming language barriers, and people with disabilities will need help with accessibility.

Every library differs, so that DEIA practices will depend on the community's needs. However, some general DEIA principles can be applied in any setting. First and foremost, in creating an environment, it is vital that everyone feels welcome and respected. This could mean training staff on how to serve users in a way sensitive to their culture, making policies that encourage inclusion, and ensuring the physical space is open to everyone. Collections and programs should reflect the different people in the community.

Cultivating Empathy through Practice

In the long run, cultivating empathy through repeated practice can help us provide a better experience for our user community. Suppose you are a librarian or someone who works in library marketing, and you need help understanding the experiences of various people. In that case, it is possible that you are not aware of the biases and prejudices that you hold. You might not mean to, but your policies, procedures, services, or resources could make the marginalization that already exists worse. Empathy is critical to planning library strategies to help you solve DEIA problems. A deep understanding of the experiences, needs, and expectations of people from all backgrounds can help ensure library policies, services, and resources are as inclusive as possible.

Library marketing with empathy is a tool for understanding library users' perspectives and creating campaigns that bring out the library's unique value. Empathy helps library marketing move beyond the number of library visits and into the whys behind them. After all, behind every library card is a unique individual with an individual story—one that library marketers should strive to understand through more extraordinary acts of empathy. By developing an empathetic mindset, library marketers can ensure everyone's voices are included in decision-making processes, breaking down barriers and promoting cross-cultural understanding.

Tailor Your Empathic Marketing Approach to DEIA Values

There are three steps to developing library marketing strategies that are tailored to promoting an empathic approach to DEIA values:
- Create library services and programs that reflect diverse needs.
- Develop approaches that ensure equitable access.
- Engage in meaningful conversations with stakeholders.

Step one: Create library services and programs that reflect the community's diverse needs. These may include attending targeted events such as cultural festivals and other community gatherings, collaborating with community library partners, and launching library campaigns on social media focusing on diverse authors and topics. Also, this may involve offering classes or workshops on topics such as language learning or computer coding for those who may still need access to these resources. It could also include setting up special events aimed at marginalized groups within the community, such as women or people of color. These events could include panel discussions on issues affecting these groups or other educational activities designed specifically for them. By doing this, libraries can show their commitment to diversity while providing valuable resources to members of their community who may not have had access otherwise.

Step two: Develop approaches that ensure equitable access to resources and opportunities. This could involve setting up an online lending system so people can borrow books from home without physically entering the library. Additionally, libraries should evaluate their current collection policies and practices to identify gaps in the availability of materials related to marginalized communities or underserved populations. By doing this, libraries can ensure everyone has equal access to all available materials, regardless of their economic status or other factors that might prevent them from taking advantage of specific resources.

Step three: Engage in meaningful conversations with stakeholders to ensure everyone's voice is heard. This could involve hosting listening sessions with members of underserved populations within the local area or inviting experts from different backgrounds onto panels at events hosted by the library. It could also involve reaching out directly via social media platforms like Twitter or Instagram to ask for feedback on the most beneficial programming for specific demographics within the community. By doing this, libraries can create a more inclusive environment where everyone feels welcome and valued, regardless of their background or identity.

Addressing DEIA Values

The best ways to address your library's DEIA needs will vary depending on your library's outreach service needs. The following are some common ways to promote DEIA values in your library, but this list is not exhaustive:

- Review library policies and procedures to ensure they are fair and equitable for all users.
- Offer training and professional development opportunities on diversity, equity, inclusion, and accessibility topics.
- Create user-friendly resources focusing on inclusivity and accessibility (e.g., library guides for people with disabilities).
- Partner with community organizations to offer programs and services that reflect the community's needs.
- Diversify collections to reflect the experiences of people of color and other marginalized groups. This includes selecting materials written by authors from various racial and ethnic backgrounds and books that openly discuss race and racism.
- Provide programming and training opportunities on racism, white privilege, and allyship topics. This might include workshops, book clubs, or lectures from guest speakers.
- Seek feedback from community members about how the library can become more inclusive.
- Assess your current situation. What demographic groups are currently represented within your library or outreach service? How well are they served? What could be improved?
- Develop a diversity statement. This statement should say how committed you are to helping everyone in your community, your hiring practices, and what steps you'll take to ensure everyone has equal access to your resources and services.
- Review your policies and procedures. Please make sure they're inclusive and non-biased.
- Make sure that the staff is knowledgeable about different cultures, and they should be aware of their personal biases and work to overcome them. Libraries that invest in staff education on cultural competency will successfully create library spaces where everyone feels welcome.
- Programs and events should be planned with diversity in mind; everyone should feel welcome to attend.
- Partner with local schools, businesses, and other institutions to implement antiracism initiatives in their communities.

- Practice self-evaluation with a diversity and equity officer, librarian, committee, or outside consultant. Sometimes, your institution has an office of diversity and inclusion that provides training.
- A crucial part of sustaining DEIA initiatives is ensuring that library efforts remain effective and impactful. Library administrators should take extra care to review them cyclically. A quarterly or biannual review conducted by an outside group or DEIA committee can be valuable for gauging library marketing performance regarding DEIA values, as it helps library managers identify any potential areas for improvement or update strategies as needed.
- Use ALA's Diversity Committee DEIA Scorecard by Natisha Harper, Kimberly Y. Franklin, and Jamia Williams to assess your practices.

The Takeaway: Bridging the Gap between Libraries and Diverse Audiences

Libraries play an essential role in society by providing tangible and intangible resources tailored toward connecting users with information sources, increasing knowledge acquisition, and facilitating intercultural understanding. Libraries must recognize specific demographics when it comes to library marketing. By using empathy as a tool for marketing strategies aimed at bridging the gap between libraries and diverse audiences, libraries can create meaningful relationships that foster mutual respect between people of different backgrounds while encouraging individuals to explore resources available through their local library system, ultimately leading them on paths toward knowledge acquisition and cultural understanding.

When you are open-minded and prioritize empathy in your conversations, you can create more effective marketing solutions that don't just focus on one group of people but rather benefit all users equally. By investing time and effort into cultivating open-mindedness and prioritizing empathy in library conversations, creating effective library marketing solutions that cater to all library users equally is achievable. By understanding the principles of DEIA, library professionals can develop compassionate and empathetic library marketing practices built with the needs, wants, and interests of all library patrons in mind, not just a select group of library users. With the help of additional resources and continually refining library marketing practices toward inclusivity, libraries can see promising results for positively adjusting their marketing initiatives for every user.

CHAPTER 3

Empathic Design:
A Human-centered Solution

"We can't solve problems by using the same kind of thinking we used when we created them." – Albert Einstein

Empathy is the first step in design thinking, but it is also a process in its own right—empathic design. Empathic design is like painting with a broad brush, providing a holistic perspective that considers the user's needs and expectations. Library marketing is like finetuning the details, making sure each marketing message engages the user and encourages them to act. The concept of empathic design originated in the world of UX design.

Empathic design is making resources, services, or products that focus on users' needs, motivations, and feelings and how to meet them. This type of design puts the user at the center of the design process. It is an approach that seeks to create a more personalized user experience and create resources and services that are user-centric and emotionally meaningful. Once you understand your users' needs well, you can develop marketing strategies to meet and solve those needs.

The creative process of empathic design is invaluable when it comes to problem-solving. It's often used to find new ideas, develop innovative solutions, or determine how your library could improve by noticing things others might have missed.

The empathic design process is similar to what I've done in my library marketing efforts. Since I've worked in library promotion and outreach for nearly a decade, applying empathy-driven design practices was a natural next step. As an outreach librarian, one of my primary responsibilities is actively seeking new ways to engage with one's local community and publicize the library's services. Additionally, I am responsible for promoting the library's programs and events.

Empathy is a critical component of my marketing strategy. I put myself in the shoes of my users and try to understand their needs and wants. What kind of information are they looking for? What kinds of events would they be interested in? How can I make the library more accessible and user-friendly? When I see things from their perspective, I create marketing materials and programs more likely to resonate with them.

These marketing initiatives might not always be called "empathtic design," but they typically follow a similar process, such as gathering user feedback and adjusting the marketing campaigns accordingly. Even though I didn't know it at first, I had already followed the five steps of empathic design without even realizing it. I did some research because I thought I'd discovered something new in library marketing and outreach. Finally, I came across Leonard and Rayport's "Spark Innovation Through Empathic Design." The empathic design process was like the methods I used to create marketing and outreach plans and strategies. So, when I read the five steps of empathic design, I knew they could be used to develop "a set of techniques" or criteria for creating empathic library marketing, outreach, and UX (Leonard and Rayport 1997, 103). This article helped me validate my approach to marketing and outreach for my library and gave me a name for it: "empathic design."

Empathic Design Explained

Empathic design is "about understanding people's psychological and emotional needs" (Landwehr, 2007, p. 1). Empathic design is a vital part of user-centered design and can be used in any field, including library marketing. Empathic design can help you develop empathic marketing plans and other solutions by helping you figure out what your users want and their pain points. Using empathic design principles, you can learn more about your users and create more effective marketing campaigns that speak to them. "It is possible to use [the empathic design process] on a large or small scale as a low-cost, user-centered strategy that is powerful enough to stimulate inventive changes …to reach all," wrote Anne Marie Perrault and Aimee M. Levesque in Knowledge Quest (2012, p. 17).

Using empathic design can help you update the strategic plan for your library and meet the needs of a wide range of users. Empathic design can help you narrow down what needs to be changed, whether it's a minor remodel of study space to make it more comfortable for the users or creating training materials that better explain how the library works. Empathic design involves observing, taking notes, thinking and analyzing, coming up with ideas for solutions, and making prototypes (Leonard and Rayport, 1997). This way of ideating is based on the idea that people are social animals who want to connect, and that connection works best when it considers each person's needs and emotions and responds to how people act. It also has implications for library marketing and outreach since libraries are all about meeting the needs of their users. Empathic design is also a great way to understand *why* people use (or don't use) library services.

Using empathic design can help you deepen empathy and understand the struggles that people with different backgrounds face when accessing information and using the library. Putting empathy into the user experience means using a user-centered approach in everything you do; from the resources and services you offer to the programs and events you plan. Knowing our users and what they require from us requires time and effort. Then, you can develop genuinely novel solutions that enhance their experience.

Why is Empathic Design Important?

Empathic design is an integral part of making user-centered campaigns and solutions, and it can be used in any industry, including libraries. Additionally, empathic design can help you avoid potential problems before they arise that might otherwise lead to user frustration or even cause churn. Being open to feedback and willing to make changes based on what your users tell you will show them that you value their input. These factors will lead to a more successful library marketing strategy overall. Doing so can improve the user experience and make your marketing and outreach efforts more effective. Empathic design is an essential tool that doesn't cost much and doesn't pose much risk. Also, the empathic design process can make it easier for people inside and outside the library to work together to develop strategic, empathic marketing, communications, social media, outreach, and educational materials. So, when you plan your next project or campaign, use empathic design to ensure you're meeting your users' needs.

Empathic Design in Library Marketing

I first used empathic design in creating personas, which I found very useful, so I incorporated it into my marketing strategies and other communication-based plans. Sometime into my time as an outreach librarian, I realized that I had automatically put myself in the shoes of our users when developing library marketing and outreach tactics because I wanted to get the word out about the library to a group that traditional outreach methods don't usually reach. This is where empathic design came in.

Empathic design can help you learn more about how users act, which can help with everything from strategic planning to marketing, considering not just what users say they need but also their unspoken needs. You can more effectively communicate the value of your services and show them how the library can meet their needs in a way they may not have even considered.

You can use empathic design in many ways when creating marketing materials. One way is to conduct user research. This can be done through surveys, interviews, focus groups, or casual conversations with users. A second way to use empathic design in your library's marketing is to make sure that all of your materials can be used by anyone who wants to use them by considering age, ability level, language barriers, etc.

For example, let's say you are developing a marketing campaign for your library's new e-book collection. You begin by surveying your users to find out what books they are interested in reading. Based on survey results, you select titles that you think would appeal to your user base. Then, you use a series of targeted emails and social media posts to get the word out about the collection. By marketing with empathy, you will be able to meet your users' needs better and bring more attention to the e-books in your library.

Additionally, empathic design can be used to evaluate existing marketing materials for the e-book collections. Are they meeting the needs of your audience? If not, how can they be improved? In the end, this will help you develop a better way to market your library. Always be open to feedback and willing to make changes based on what your users tell you. After all, they're the ones who matter most!

Creating Messages That Resonate

You can use empathic design to create marketing campaigns with messages that are more likely to resonate with users and that they are more likely to find useful. Here are some general tips that may be useful:

- Develop marketing materials that are visually appealing and easy to understand.
- Make sure that all communications are clear and concise.
- Get to know your users through surveys and focus groups.
- Understand their needs and pain points.
- Design your marketing messages and materials accordingly.

Empathic Design Steps

If you follow empathic design principles to the letter, you can be sure that your library's marketing is truly user-centered. We can create more powerful campaigns that change things by putting users first, and creating services and spaces that meet their wants and needs. The empathic design process is broken down into five steps:

Empathic Design Process

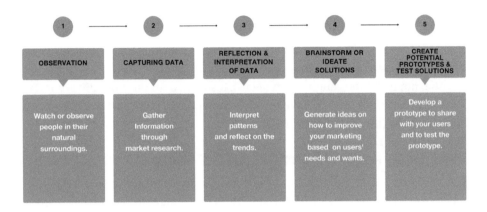

Figure 3. The five steps of the empathic design process.

- Step 1: Observation
- Step 2: Capturing data
- Step 3: Reflection and interpretation of data
- Step 4: Brainstorm or ideate solutions
- Step 5: Create potential prototypes and test solutions

Let's take a closer look at each step.

Step 1: Observation

To understand how your users use your resources and services and to gain empathy for them, you need to watch them in their natural environment. It's important to take note of both their positive and negative interactions. This will help you identify any pain points they may have so that you can address them in the next step.

Step 2: Capturing Data

Once you have made your observations, it's time to capture data based on them. Data capture is the process of collecting information about your users so that you can understand them better. This information can come from several places, such as surveys, interviews with users, user testing, and even analytics data from websites and programming surveys.

Step 3: Reflection and Interpretation of Data

In the reflection and interpretation phase, you will learn more about your users by determining what the data you gathered in the first two steps means. During this phase, looking for patterns and trends in your data is important to understand your users' needs and wants.

Step 4: Brainstorm or Ideate Solutions

Now, it's time to start generating ideas for improving your marketing based on what you've learned about your users' needs and wants. During this phase, it's essential not to get too caught up in details; instead, focus on generating as many ideas as possible. Once you have multiple viewpoints, you can start narrowing them down in the next phase.

Step 5: Create Potential Prototypes and Test Solutions

The final phase of the empathic design process is prototyping and testing. In this two-part phase, you will take the ideas that emerged from the previous step, develop a prototype to share with your users, and put it to the test by implementing it as a marketing solution on a trial basis. After testing, take note of what works and what doesn't so that you can further improve your solution.

You'll read more about each of these steps in the following chapters.

Achieving Resource/Program/Service "Nirvana"

If you use the empathic design process, you can be sure that your solutions will be tailored to the needs of your users. A well-designed plan can efficiently execute the empathic design process, resulting in a more satisfying user experience. This, in turn, can lead to valuable feedback and insights for further design process improvement. After launching your campaign, listen to what real users say and, if necessary, keep testing with them. Refine your feedback based on what users say, make changes as needed, and then repeat the process as often as required until marketing your resource, program, or service succeeds. This kind of success—I call it "Nirvana"—happens when most or all the users who have a stake in the resource, program, or service are happy with it. The goal of the empathic design process is to reach a state of "Nirvana," where the resource, program, or service perfectly meets the needs of its users. Achieving this goal requires patience, dedication, and a willingness to listen to and act on user feedback.

Achieving resource/program/service "Nirvana" is an ambitious but attainable goal reached through hard work, problem-solving ability, and a dedication to excellence. Doing so requires an in-depth understanding of user problems, the resources available, and how those resources can be used to create a successful outcome. It is a process that needs to be carefully planned, carried out, and constantly improved as new customer needs arise. The goal is to match resources, programs, and services with user wants and needs while staying within budget constraints.

To make a marketing prototype that meets users' expectations, you need to plan well, choose the right tools, and use what you've learned in the previous stages. By taking a second look at your existing resources, introducing new programs, and providing user-centric services, you can maximize the offerings for a successful result. To ensure high-quality prototyping throughout the process, contributors inside the library (staff members, librarians) and outside the library (users, community members) must focus on continuous improvement and open communication.

The Takeaway: Empathtic Design in Action

When it comes to problem-solving, the creative process of empathic design is an invaluable, powerful tool. It's often used to find new opportunities, come up with innovative solutions, or figure out how your library could be better by spotting things that might have been missed. Where traditional marketing methods might fail to consider the needs of the people they are attempting to reach, empathic design is all about understanding the needs and desires of users and then using that information to create resources or services that meet those needs. By following the five steps listed—defining your user, doing research, interpreting the data (by making user representations like personas), creating a strategy, testing, and iterating—you can make a marketing campaign that will reach and engage your target audience meaningfully.

Here's an example of how empathic design can be used to create a marketing campaign that will reach and interest your target audience:

Define Your User through Observation

Who are you trying to reach with your marketing campaign? What are their needs? Be as specific as possible when answering these questions. Once you've defined your user, it's time to do some research. Talk to people who fit your target demographic and find out what they're looking for in a library or similar institution. You can also look at surveys, reference transactions, or social media data to better understand your users' needs.

Create Representations of the Data

Once you've gathered your research, it's time to create representations of the data. My favorite ways to make representations of the data is to develop personas or journey maps. Personas are fictional characters that represent your target users. Journey maps break the overall user experience down into steps. These representations should be based on actual data and include demographics, goals, pain points, and how they might interact with your library or institution. Creating personas, journey maps, and more can be overwhelming for librarians who are newer to user experience. Still, it will help you focus your marketing efforts and ensure your campaigns reach your target audience.

Develop Marketing Strategies and Plans

Now that you know who you're targeting and what they need, it's time to develop marketing strategies that will reach them where they are. This might involve creating new content, redesigning your website, or using different channels to promote your library or institution. Whatever strategy you choose, ensure it aligns with your goals and is feasible within your budget.

Test and Iterate

Finally, once you've launched your marketing campaign, testing it and seeing how it performs is important. Collect user feedback, record it, evaluate it, and make necessary changes. Empathic design is an ongoing process, so be prepared to iterate on your strategy as needed based on user feedback.

References

Landwehr, P. (2207). "Empathic design vs. empathetic design: A history of confusion." *Lab 3, 1–4.*
Perrault, A. M., & Levesque, A. M. (2012). "Caring for all students: empathic design as a driver for innovative school library services and programs." *Knowledge Quest* 40, no. 5, 16–18.

CHAPTER 4

Observation and Identifying the Needs of Users

"Libraries are about more than books. They're about community, understanding, and empathy. They're a symbol of our commitment to the Bill of Rights and the free exchange of ideas. We must do everything we can to support them." – Barack Obama

Figure 4. The five steps of the empathic design process begin with observation.

In the first step of empathic design, marketers observe users to discover their needs and experiences. This step helps marketers understand users' perspectives and develop empathy. Observation allows users to say what they think about why they use libraries and what they think are the downsides of using libraries. Also, observation provides insight into users' needs and desires when using the library. Once you understand the user's experience, you can observe their behavior directly. This can be done through shadowing, ethnographic research, or simply following users in the virtual or physical environment. Leonard and Rayport (1997) explain that the observation step in empathic design can help "yield at least five types of information that cannot be gathered through traditional marketing research: triggers of use, interactions with the user's environment, user customization, intangible attributes of the resource, and unarticulated user needs" (Leonard and Rayport, 1997, pp. 106–107).

By observing users, we can learn how they interact with our libraries. This information can help us develop marketing campaigns that are more effective and user-friendly. Empathic design helps to clarify "who should be observed, who should be doing the observing, and what the observer should be watching" (Leonard and Rayport 1997, p. 108). The observation step is critical because it allows researchers to see how people use the resource or service for themselves. Those watching should pay attention to verbal and nonverbal cues and write down users' problems or frustrations.

When you watch users in their natural environment, you can learn important things that will help you make campaigns that work better. Observe people using the library and take note of anything that seems difficult or frustrating. This will help you learn how people interact with their environment in the library, and you can look for ways to improve things. Interact with real users in the library to learn about who they are and what they do to get a complete picture of the user. Marketers with empathy should talk to their users as much as possible and not just rely on user studies or survey data to learn about them. You can directly observe users in the library, either in person or by studying video footage or other records. Watch users do tasks and carefully note their actions, facial expressions, and body language. This process can also help find potential pain points or places where people are frustrated. This knowledge makes creating campaigns that better meet users' needs possible. Without it, it is too easy to develop solutions that are out of touch with the realities of the people using them.

When doing observations for empathic design, it's essential to know who should be observed. This will typically be the target audience for the designed resource or service. Second, it is crucial to decide who will be doing the observing. In many situations, it may be helpful to use a team of observers to learn more about how users act and to avoid bias, whether conscious or unconscious. Furthermore, it would be best to establish what resource, service, or program precisely should be observed. This may include user interactions with the resource or service, body language, emotions, tone of voice, and facial expressions. To analyze the observations and use them to guide the design process, it will be essential to ensure they are written down.

In the observation step of empathic design, you can find out about "triggers of use," "interactions with the user's environment," "user customization," "intangible attributes of the resource," and "unarticulated user needs" (Leonard and Rayport 1997). Let's examine the five different types of information about users that the observation step will generate.

Triggers of Use

What made you use the library today?
So, what motivations, behaviors, and circumstances led someone to use (or not use) our library? The library is a resource of information and support that many people rely on, and marketers can make more effective campaigns by knowing what leads people to use a resource. Triggers of use make us want to use a particular resource or attend a specific program or event—in this case, using the library. People interacting with the library often do so in response to one or more triggers of use.

However, the library can also be a source of frustration for users. This is often because library professionals or resources can only sometimes meet some users' needs. In addition, the library may only occasionally have the funds to provide the resources their users need. As a result, it is essential to understand what triggers the use of the library and how users interact with the library environment. Triggers of use are an integral part of observation. Triggers can come from the outside (like an ad or a post on social media) or from the inside (like being bored).

Three specific triggers can be used to market with empathy: social connection, self-expression, and playfulness. By incorporating these triggers into your marketing strategies, you can create a more empathic connection with your audience and better understand their needs. Social connection refers to people's need to belong and to feel connected to others, such as when library users feel like they belong or are part of a community. Self-expression triggers empathy by allowing people to express themselves and be seen and heard, like when they can express themselves in the library or through the library's resources. Playfulness can provide fun and relaxation where the user can explore and experiment.

Everyone's triggers for using the library might differ, but they must first be aware that it even exists. Personal invitations to the library and recommendations from people they know, and trust can also be influential. Outreach programs can have a greater reach if they focus on marketing, advertising, and making library use appear as easy and accessible as possible. Appealing to common triggers regarding convenience, relevance, familiarity, and word-of-mouth recommendations will likely increase users' engagement with the library. For some, a trigger is simply being aware of the library's resources and potential usefulness. Another trigger might be receiving a personal invitation or recommendation to use the resource from someone they know and trust. Still, others may be prompted to use the resource in response to advertising or publicity. And finally, some people may be more likely to use the resource if it is convenient and easy to access. Triggers of use can vary greatly from individual to individual but understanding them is key to designing effective marketing and outreach programs for libraries and other public institutions.

Case Study: Need a Quiet Place to Study

My motivation (trigger for use) for using the library was the need for a quiet place to study. I have found that the library is the perfect place for me to focus on my work and get away from distractions. I usually go to the same spot in the library, set up my laptop, and get to work. I know where everything is, and I can easily find what I need. The staff is also very friendly and helpful if I need anything.

User customization is another important factor in why I continue to use the library. As my needs change, I can adjust my use of the library accordingly. When I was working on a group project, for example, I needed to use a lot of different resources and meeting rooms. Finally, the intangible aspects of the library make it a great environment to focus on my work; its peaceful atmosphere helps get me in the right mindset to be resourceful and effective with my studies.

Interactions with the User's Environment

How did they use the library?

When marketing a library, it's important to think about the user's environment when creating empathic solutions. The library user's environment includes factors such as their age, library location, and how the user interacts with the library. For example, a library user who is a senior citizen might have different needs than a library user who is a college student, like the one mentioned in the example above. A library user who lives in a rural area might have different needs than a library user who lives in an urban area. As a result, libraries allow marketers to create resources that help these people learn and find new things.

To fully understand how a library fits into the users' environment, one must first understand what an "idiosyncratic system" is (Leonard & Rayport 1997, p. 106). Leonard and Rayport (1997) explain that an idiosyncratic system is a set of unique activities and relationships that are hard to copy by other users. In other words, it is unique to every individual. Each person has their way of doing things, and the library must be able to adapt to that. For example, some people prefer to read print books, while others prefer e-books. The library must be able to provide both to cater to all types of users. In addition, the library must also be able to interact with the user's other systems, such as their school or work.

It is not enough for the library to just exist; it must be integrated into the user's life for it to be truly effective.

User Customization

How do they customize their use of the library?
Do your users "reinvent or redesign" for their purposes? (Leonard & Rayport 1997, 106). Leonard and Rayport (1997, p. 106) explain that "user customization" is when a person changes or adapts a resource or service to better fit their needs. This can be done in many ways, such as by changing the way something is used or by adding new features. For example, they may create personalized reading lists or use the library's online catalog in a unique way that meets their specific needs. Others may "reinvent or redesign" the library's services for their reasons, like making a new way to track when books are due or making the online catalog easier to use.

User customization is a broad term that can encompass a variety of activities. Some users, for example, might just change how they use the library by choosing which resources to use and when. Others may take a more proactive approach, actively seeking out ways to make the library work better for them. This could mean anything from giving feedback to the library professionals to changing or making up new rules for the library. Users sometimes may even "reinvent or redesign" the library for their purposes. While this latter approach is not always possible or practical, it highlights that user customization is often about more than just individual preferences; it can also be about finding ways to improve the library.

Changing how a resource looks and works for each user can make it easier for people to use and make it less likely that they will get frustrated with library resources. Libraries offer a wide range of customization options that can be used to create a unique user experience. For example, libraries can be used to customize the color scheme of a resource or to add or remove features based on the user's needs. Libraries can also be used to make detailed profiles of users that can be used to make personalized suggestions or recommendations. By taking advantage of user customization libraries, we can create resources that are better able to meet the needs of our users.

Intangible Attributes of the Library

How do they feel after using the library today? Accomplished? Dissatisfied?
Library marketing is not just about promoting the services and resources that are available. It's also about getting the word out about the library's less tangible

qualities, like its role as a place for people to get together, its commitment to intellectual freedom, and its reputation as a reliable source of information. By highlighting these attributes, library marketing can help build public support and ensure that the library remains an essential part of the community.

The marketing team of a library tries to show the community it serves how valuable the library is. To do this effectively, they must first understand which library resources are most important to users. Some library users may care about how many books or journals are available, but others may care more about how the library makes them feel. These can include the quality of the reference service, the friendliness of the staff, or the comfortable atmosphere of the library. When you know what users care about most, you can ensure that your communication plans focus on the library's best features. As a result, the library can more effectively demonstrate its value to the community and attract new users. Emphasizing the library's role as a quiet study space, a safe haven, and a helpful resource center can help show users how the library can benefit them academically and emotionally.

Unarticulated User Needs

Is there anything that the library could do better to meet your needs?
What does the library need to improve to reach the user? Most library marketing focuses on telling people about the library's current services and resources. But library marketers must also be aware of the needs of their community's users that aren't being expressed. Unarticulated user needs are the wants and desires of library users that they may need to be made aware of. For example, a library user may need to learn how to request books through the interlibrary loan system or get help citing sources from a reference librarian. By understanding the unarticulated user needs of their community, library marketers can provide users with the information and resources they need, even before they know they need them. In other words, users may need to be made aware of the services and resources that would be most helpful to them. This is where library marketing comes in. By publicizing the library's offerings and raising awareness of what the library can do, library marketing can help meet unarticulated user needs. Library marketing can also help build relationships with potential users who may not be aware of the library's value.

Understanding Pain Points

A "pain point" is defined as any source of frustration that leads users to not use a resource, service, or system. In the context of libraries, pain points can include everything from not being able to find a quiet spot to study to feeling anxious about using the library itself. Library anxiety is a particularly common problem, and it can be triggered by a number of different factors, including previous bad experiences, feelings of insecurity, and fear of judgment. While addressing pain points can be difficult, it is essential to ensure that users have a positive experience with the library. By identifying and addressing the various triggers of use, libraries can create an environment that is welcoming and inclusive for all. For example, one user commented in a survey that was conducted that "the library hours were too short. Most universities have the library open until 1 a.m. or later." The CIO observed to the library director that we should have a section on the library hours sign on the door about alternative study spaces on campus that were open 24/7. This was developed with the express purpose of meeting and empathizing with this user's pain point during library hours.

Identifying User Motivations

It can take much work to determine user behavior, preferences, and motivations, especially in marketing. Observation also provides valuable insights into user behavior, preferences, and motivations. In general, observational research is more likely to lead to results that a larger group of people can use. When doing marketing research for a library, it is often helpful to look at library users' overall trends and patterns of behavior. However, there are some potential issues with this kind of data collection. For example, because it is observational, there is no control group and no ability to measure the actual outcome. The results can be understood more by what was seen when the respondents were being watched than by what they did. This can make it difficult to draw conclusions about causation or predict future behavior. Researchers can see users in action, unscripted and unfiltered when they watch them in their natural environment.

Ethnographic studies are also helpful for evaluating existing services and resources. For example, an ethnographic study could be used to evaluate an existing service or resource by observing how people use it and then analyzing the data collected from the study. It tells us things we couldn't find out from a survey or focus group. Also, watching users in their natural environment can help develop new ideas and solutions that could improve the events, resources, or services. Even people who use services or resources often find it hard to explain what's wrong. For example, suppose you and your team are designing a new website. Rather than simply asking users what they want in a new website, observing them while using the current website would be more effective. This will help you identify areas where they are struggling and understand the thought process behind their actions.

In general, observational research is more likely to lead to results that a larger group of people can use when it leads to an understanding of the overall trends and patterns of behavior among library users.

Other factors can affect library marketing research results. For example, you may see limited results if you are trying to collect data in an area with limited exposure to your brand or a limited budget for your research efforts. The type of data collection method can also make a big difference. For example, web surveys can be very quick and easy to set up, but they may not yield the same level of detail and accuracy as in-person interviews or focus groups.

The Takeaway: Observation and Identification of the Needs of Users

Another thing to remember is that any observational research is, by definition, qualitative research. This means that it must offer easy figures about how effective your library marketing campaign will be. The best way to measure the effectiveness of your library marketing campaign is through in-person research like focus groups and surveys, which I discuss in Chapter 5, Capturing Data.

Library users' thoughts and experiences should be considered when making services that meet their needs. By observing users, you may identify individuals who would otherwise go unnoticed. Keeping in mind that observation is the basis of empathic design, you can create a user-centered library that works well and is easy for people to use. For example, you may want to observe how users search for books and other materials, browse the shelves, and check out materials. You can also observe how people use the library website, contact library professionals, and receive services. Through these observations, you can collect data about your users' demographics, needs, and preferences and determine how to adjust your marketing strategies accordingly.

Finding the right people to observe can take time and effort. One way to do this is to set up focus groups. Ask people what they want from your library and what they struggle with. You might also want to look at other data sources to find your target audience. This may include surveys, interviews, and polls where you can ask people about their preferences. Once you've found a possible user group, you should watch how they use your resource and write down any problems you see. Once you've done this for a few user groups, you should combine all your observations and create a list of issues that you see being faced by your users.

With this list, you should imagine possible solutions and create a roadmap to solve these issues. According to Kathy Dempsey, author of "Accidental Library Marketer," many librarians create events and services for their users that they weren't even asked for, wasting valuable resources. It would be better to focus on observing your users and designing based on what you see rather than on what you believe they want. Through empathic design's observational process, you can build a more accessible library for your users. This is significant because it will allow you to construct a more inclusive and welcoming library.

References

Dempsey, K. (2009). Accidental library marketer. *Information Today.*
Leonard, D., & Rayport, J. F. (1997). "Spark innovation through empathic design." *Harvard Business Review,* 75, 102–115.

CHAPTER 5

Gathering Accurate, Reliable Data for Informed Decisions

"I do believe that libraries are citadels of knowledge and empathy." – Barack Obama

Figure 5. Capturing data is the second step in the empathtic design process.

The second step in the empathic design process is capturing data through market research. Capturing data is a key marketing tool that will help you understand your users. As libraries rely more and more on data to make decisions, they must think about how this data can be used to improve their marketing and outreach by gaining a better understanding of the target audience. What are their needs and interests? What motivates them to use the library? By learning more about your audience, you can create marketing campaigns and outreach programs that are more likely to reach them and make an impact. This chapter is not meant to be an exhaustive list of all things related to market research; rather, it is simply a brief guide for those working with market research as part of their job responsibilities.

Empathic design in the capturing data step involves considering the users' subjective experience. In library marketing, you can use empathic design to gain insight into the user's perception of a library through data collection, such as user interactions, user feedback, and usage patterns. When capturing data in the empathic design process, it's important to consider the user's feelings and emotions. You can use various techniques to gather this data, such as user interviews, surveys, and focus groups. By understanding the user's needs and wants, you can create effective marketing and design strategies and help you improve user experience and interface. These data can then inform decisions about the library itself and its services. For example, if there is evidence that users are dissatisfied with the library's layout, this could prompt graphic design changes to improve the experience for users.

Empathic design requires libraries to take a user-centered approach to service design, which can be difficult to do in practice. However, several tools and methods can help librarians better understand the needs of their users. Identifying the needs of your users is a multilayered task that cannot be accomplished with one technique. User surveys, focus groups, and user observation are all excellent ways to gather data about user needs and experiences. The most common ways to identify latent desires or psychological states in people would involve interviewing real users, doing creative brainstorming sessions where you ask different types of questions, and conducting user surveys.

Data can also be used to track how well your marketing campaigns are working and allow you to make any changes that are needed. Are certain campaigns generating more interest than others? Are there specific times of year when engagement is higher? You can make sure that your marketing and outreach efforts are user-centered by constantly evaluating and changing how you do things. You can divide your audience into groups with the help of data, which makes marketing more targeted and effective. Also, data can help you figure out which programs and services are most popular with users. This lets you tailor your services to better meet the needs of the community. Lastly, data can help libraries figure out which groups they are not currently reaching so they can make plans to reach out to those groups.

Data capture allows you to understand your users on a deeper level—to learn about their motivators, goals, pain points, and much more. This information is essential for informed decision-making when it comes to marketing strategy. With it, you can make choices that are based on real data instead of guesses, biases, or assumptions. The value of data capture lies in the ability to gain insight into user behavior and preferences. By collecting information on how users interact with your resource, you can analyze trends and adjust to better meet their needs, creating a resource that is tailored specifically to your users' wants and needs.

Furthermore, data capture allows you to track changes over time so you can measure the impact of design choices and identify opportunities for improvement. With this knowledge, you can optimize resources, programs, and services for maximum efficiency and satisfaction. Additionally, data capture is invaluable for preventing errors in development processes. By observing usage patterns and metrics, you can catch issues before they become major problems down the line. Finally, data capture enables you to collect feedback from your users quickly and accurately, which leads to improved user retention rates and overall satisfaction. This lets you make changes quickly based on what you learn from real users' feedback, which makes it easier to keep users and makes them happier overall. This information can be used to improve resource design, prevent mistakes in the development process, improve services, and get accurate feedback from users quickly.

Once you have this data, you can create a profile of your users and their needs to help design new library services and events to better serve their communities. This can be helpful for libraries because it can help them figure out where users are having trouble. For example, if the data shows that users are having difficulty finding specific items, the library can make changes to its layout or signage. You can also use data to test your designs to see how users react to different designs and to see which designs are more effective.

Also, after users have used your resource or service, you can ask for their feedback. In the world of data capture, empathic design can be a big help in making sure that we get accurate and trustworthy information that shows how the user really feels. Accurate and reliable information is vital in order to draw valid conclusions. To ensure that your data is of the highest quality, here are some tips for capturing it:

- **Design a clear and concise plan.** Create a plan for gathering data that outlines each step you need to take to get the results you need. Make sure it is clear, concise, and covers every necessary element of your project.
- **Use multiple sources.** Collecting data from multiple sources will give you more comprehensive results. Consider using surveys, interviews, observations, and other methods such as analyzing existing documents.
- **Keep quality in mind.** Quality is key when it comes to data collection. Make sure that all questions or instructions used in surveys or interviews are accurate, easy to understand, and written in neutral language so as not to introduce bias into the responses.
- **Investigate and verify data points.** Before making any definitive statements based on collected data, always investigate and verify individual data points for accuracy. This will help ensure that your results are reliable and can be trusted.
- **Save your results.** Make sure all your gathered information is stored securely with appropriate backup measures in case of accidental loss or damage. This will help protect your findings so they can be reviewed and analyzed at a later date if needed.

Let's Talk About Market Research

Market research is an important tool for understanding our users and the needs of our community. Marketing research is a branch of marketing that looks at how users perceive and respond to services, resources, or, in some cases, products. Market research can also help you understand how users act and what they like, as well as find ways to make the resource or service better. It provides insight into how people think, feel, and behave. We use this knowledge to improve programs, services, and resources that meet the needs of our users. This is because capturing data can provide insights into people's real-world needs and behaviors. For example, it can help to understand how people interact with each other, what they find frustrating, and what they find valuable.

Market research data can also help identify patterns in people's thoughts and feelings. This can then be used to create more effective designs that are better aligned with people's needs and wants. Additionally, gathering data in a respectful and considerate way for the user is essential. Some best practices for capturing data in an empathic design include

- asking the user what their goals and needs are;
- gathering data in a respectful and considerate manner;
- considering the user's context when gathering data;
- analyzing the data in a way that is sensitive to the user's needs and
- collecting data collection by various methods, from interviews and surveys to user testing, focus groups, and observations.

Every method has advantages and disadvantages, so it's crucial to select the one that suits your needs the best. The fact that it offers insight into the requirements and preferences of your target market is what matters most. For example, interviews only give insights into how individuals feel and think and may not be representative of a wider population. Surveys can provide statistical data but may be subject to self-selection bias.

Surveys are an invaluable resource for collecting market research data from library users. Through surveys, you can gain an understanding of how people perceive the library, what their pain points and needs are, and even their demographics and psychographics. Also, surveys can help you figure out how well your outreach efforts are working and where you should put your efforts next.

Interviews and taking notes may also be beneficial when it comes to gaining user insight. If you need to observe users, try asking them directly what they like and don't like about their experience with your resources or services; this method might be more useful in a focus group. In a focus group, a group of potential or current users is brought together to discuss a resource or service. Focus groups can help you find out what people think about new or possible services and how they feel about them.

It is important to use multiple methods when attempting to understand the needs of your users. The methods listed above are not the only methods available. Another option would be to use data analytics, affinity analysis, models, or usability testing to look for patterns in user behavior. These could be used in combination with other methods to get a more complete picture of what users want. They can also assist you in developing marketing plans that are tailored to the needs of the people you want to reach. By taking the time to fully understand what users want and need from their library experience, they can use this information to create marketing campaigns and plans that are centered on the users.

How to Begin Your Market Research Journey

Efficient and effective library marketing requires an understanding of your target audience and their needs. To gain such an understanding, market research can be incredibly beneficial. With empathy at its heart, you can start your market research journey by considering all the different factors that influence library users—from demographics to psychographics to their individual needs and pain points.

There are various methods of conducting market research, from shadowing and ethnographic research to simply observing users in the environment, whether virtual or physical. No single research method is perfect, and the best approach for your project will depend on your specific needs and goals. By understanding the strengths and weaknesses of each research method, you can choose the best approach for your marketing campaigns and plans. For example, if you know that a large number of your users are working mothers, you can design your outreach and programming accordingly. The best data collection method will vary depending on the situation, but all these methods can be useful for capturing user data.

Gathering User Feedback through Surveys, Focus Groups, and Interviews

One of the best ways to get started with empathic market research is to use surveys and interviews to get feedback from users. This allows you to ask direct questions about your users' needs as well as gain valuable insights into their overall experiences when using the library.

Empathic market research can also be done by using information about how users use libraries that are available from different places, such as the libraries' own databases or third-party tools. With these tools, libraries can keep track of user behavior from a variety of angles, such as usage patterns and preferred resources. This information can then be used to make decisions about marketing strategy and messaging. Furthermore, tracking user behavior with resources such as analytics tools can help frame the overall user experience while researching deeper underlying motivations. This kind of data helps paint a picture of the user experience as a whole. It can be used to figure out deeper motivations that may not have been clear from surveys or interviews alone.

Analytics Tools

While gathering user feedback and user experience, data are two important steps in conducting empathic market research for library marketing campaigns. It's also essential to consider the usage of analytics tools such as Google Analytics or Facebook Insights that allow libraries to measure success in terms of website visits, clicks, shares, and more. By tracking these metrics over time, it's possible to get a better understanding of user behavior while also determining what types of content resonate best with library users in order to tailor future messages accordingly.

Surveys

Surveys are a great way to quickly gain insight from your library's users and can help find patterns in how users act. Once you have gathered your survey data, conducting analysis can help you shape how you move forward with your library marketing strategy. Ask questions such as, "What brought you to this library? How often do you visit the library? What type of materials or services would you like to see more of?" Another kind of survey is to use social media, online search engines, and other platforms to find out what words and phrases people are using when talking about your library. This will help you figure out which keywords will get you the most traffic and interaction.

Interviews

Interviews can be used to gather more detailed information from individual users. While survey research is relatively quick and inexpensive, it can be difficult to get detailed information from users. Interviews can be more time-consuming and expensive, but they can provide more in-depth information.

Usability Testing

Usability testing can help you identify problems with your resources and learn how users interact with them. Usability testing can also be time-consuming and expensive, but it can be very helpful for identifying problems and improving resources. Once you have this information, it's important to analyze it carefully. Look for common themes and patterns that emerge during your research. This will give you a better understanding of your audience's needs and how you can best meet them. For example, a library might use heat mapping to track where users are spending the most time in the facility. This information can then be used to improve the flow of traffic or make changes to the layout of the space.

Focus Groups

Focus groups allow for in-depth and probing discussions to take place among a select group of individuals. The data that is generated from focus groups can be very rich and detailed, providing valuable insights into how users feel about the library and its services. When conducting focus groups for a library, it is important to gather input from individuals with different backgrounds and needs. For example, you might want to speak with users who use the library regularly as well as those who only visit occasionally. You might also want to consult with people from different age groups as well as those who live in different parts of the city.

To ensure that the market research is conducted effectively, it is important to carefully select the participants for the focus group and to create a conducive environment for discussion. When gathering input from library users, keep in mind that everyone's opinion is valuable. Ask open-ended questions and be prepared to listen attentively. Remember that you are not looking for a "right" answer but rather trying to get a sense of what people like and don't like about the library. You can then use this information to develop marketing plans and outreach programs that will appeal to your target audience.

Observational Reports

Observational reports are different from traditional research reports because they are created by observing a subject. These types of reports are most commonly used in libraries to report information on the collection or usage of certain books or resources. Observational reports can also be used to report statistics on the behavior of library users. In addition, observational reports can also be used to improve the efficiency, accessibility, and effectiveness of library services. Librarians can use observational reports to analyze the number of visitors to their branches and the reasons that visitors come to visit them. This knowledge can help them create marketing and outreach strategies that will encourage more people to visit their libraries. In addition, librarians can use observational reports to identify any issues users might have with the library and then work with users to develop solutions for these problems. Once you have this data, you can start to see trends and make informed decisions about your library's resources, programs, and services. These reports can be used for planning and budgeting, or they can be shared with other community leaders so that everyone is on the same page about the issues that matter most to them. In short, observational reports help you build a more effective library program by giving you a better idea of what people actually want from your library.

Remember that research is an ongoing process. You may run into problems you didn't expect, but finding solutions is part of the empathic design journey. Research is an iterative process, meaning that it's never finished. You'll probably run into unexpected roadblocks along the way, but that's okay.

Tips for Creating a Survey or Questionnaire

The purpose of a survey is to acquire information about your target audience. When conducting surveys, you can ask users to answer questions about their experience with the library and how they'd like to be able to access the library's services. This information can help you determine how well your library is meeting the needs of the community and what areas may need improvement. Also, this information can be used to develop marketing strategies, improve resource or service offerings, and evaluate current initiatives.

Survey questions are usually grouped into three categories: demographic, attitudinal, and behavioral. Creating an effective survey or questionnaire involves taking multiple considerations into account. Here are some tips to help you craft an effective survey or questionnaire that yields meaningful results:

- Determine your purpose for the survey or questionnaire. Knowing what information, you hope to gain from the survey will help guide the construction and content of the questions.
- Make sure that you have clear SMART (specific, measurable, attainable, relevant, and timely) goals in mind that will help you craft questions that are relevant and actionable.
- Create clear and concise questions that elicit precise answers. Your respondents should understand exactly what answer you are looking

for without any confusion or ambiguity. Provide easy-to-understand answer choices for each question so participants can easily understand and respond accurately. For example, if asking about frequency of usage, provide options such as "daily, monthly," etc., instead of having participants guess at their own frequency.
- Ask open-ended questions that allow respondents to provide detailed responses. Make sure that each question is concise and focused on one specific topic. Avoid multiple-part questions or overly complex phrasing, which may confuse participants or lead them to provide inaccurate answers.
- If appropriate, give participants an opportunity to provide open responses either by providing an empty field for written text or by allowing participants to choose "Other" as an option when presented with closed-choice questions. This will allow more freedom in answering while still giving definitive data points.
- Avoid leading questions such as "How likely is it that you will…" or "What do you like most about…"
- Stress the importance of providing accurate responses to your survey takers.
- Keep your questions as neutral as possible, avoiding words that could potentially trigger emotional responses or bias in their answers.
- When it comes to question order, start with easier, less intimate questions before progressing toward more difficult or sensitive topics. This can make participants feel more comfortable and open to providing honest feedback.
- Be sure to give respondents an easy way out of answering any questions they don't feel comfortable disclosing or do not wish to answer altogether. By giving them the choice, you can ensure that all collected data is accurate and relevant.
- Take the time to get input from as many people as possible so that you can create a survey that has relevance and value for your library marketing efforts.
- Make it fun when possible. Make the process enjoyable and engaging. If appropriate, add elements such as photos or videos along with audio files to break up the monotony of answering question after question. This will keep users engaged throughout the process and make it more likely that they complete the questionnaire.
- Be transparent about how the results will be used.

The Takeaway: Capturing Data and Marketing Research

There are different ways that you can go about conducting market research for a library. One way is to simply ask your users what they would like to see in the library. You can do this by putting up a suggestion box, sending out surveys, or hosting focus groups. Another way to conduct market research is to look at demographic data and try to identify trends in your community that could impact the library's services.

The first step in conducting market research for a library is to develop a clear understanding of the library's target audience. This will enable you to identify the most effective research methods and sources of information. Once you have gathered all relevant data, it is important to analyze it carefully to understand the needs and wants of your target market. You can use the data from the first two steps to make decisions about how to best serve the community. This may include expanding or changing services, marketing library services more effectively, or allocating resources differently.

Data capture is an essential part of empathic design. By collecting information about your users, you can improve your understanding of their wants and needs. This, in turn, allows you to create better resources that meet their needs more effectively. If you're not already using data capture in your marketing process, now is the time to start! During this phase, you will want to analyze your observations and make assumptions about what your users are thinking and feeling. Remember to question your assumptions so that you can ensure they are accurate and not biased. Once you have a good understanding of your users' needs, you can start developing marketing strategies and campaigns that meet those needs and solve those problems. The five ways to use data for marketing are as follows:

- To understand what your user segment is most interested in.
- To understand what communication channels they are most engaged with.
- To understand what language or messaging will resonate most with them.
- To understand what offers or incentives will be most likely to drive conversions.
- To track and measure the results of your campaign so you can optimize and improve future iterations.

CHAPTER 6

Uncovering Insights from Data:

Reflection and Interpretation

"The important thing about a problem is not the solution, but the strength we gain in finding a solution." – Seneca

Figure 6. Step three in the empathic design process is the reflection and interpretation of data.

Now that you have captured data, the next step is to analyze the data and information that you've collected. The purpose of this step is to identify patterns, trends, and insights. For example, if you've conducted a usability test, look for patterns in the participant's behavior. If they're struggling with a certain task or feature, then it's probably not very intuitive or easy to use. For example, if most of your participants are struggling with a certain task or feature because they don't understand how it works and what its purpose is, then they might need some additional explanation and/or instructions on how to use it properly. You can use this knowledge to improve programs, services, and resources that meet the needs of our users. That's why it can be deflating when a study doesn't provide any new information or uncovers something we already know. Or, even worse, what if the data in front of you is not easily understood?

Examining and Synthesizing Data from Market Research

The next step is to synthesize your findings into actionable insights and recommendations based on what you've learned from your observations and an analysis of the data that you've collected during the observation phase of the empathic design process. Then, you can present your findings and recommendations to administrators and other stakeholders in a way that's easy for them to understand and act upon. This can be done through a variety of different methods, including the following:

- A prototype (personas, empathy maps, journey maps, affinity diagramming) with annotations that illustrate your findings and recommendations.
- A presentation that explains your findings and recommendations
- A document that describes your findings and recommendations, such as an action plan and/or marketing proposal or plan.
- An interactive website that allows the stakeholders to explore and see your findings and recommendations for themselves.

It can be hard to put together the results of data and observations from market research. There are a number of different ways to approach this, and the best approach will vary depending on the specific situation. In general, though, there are a few steps that should be followed. First, all of the data and observations should be gathered in one place. This can be done manually or by using a software program specifically designed for market research. Once all of the data is gathered, it should be organized in a way that makes sense. This might involve creating charts, tables, or other visual aids, putting together a summary of the findings, and making suggestions based on the data. The main goal is to present the findings to the staff or decision-makers so they can make better decisions.

There are a number of different ways to analyze data from market research. One way is to look at the overall trends. This can be done by looking at the total number of responses for each question and comparing the results. Another way to analyze the data is to look at the responses of every individual. This can be done by looking at the responses for each question and noting any patterns or trends. Finally, it is also possible to combine the two approaches by looking at both the overall trends and the individual responses. This can give a more complete picture of the market research data. Using technology is a common method of using computer-based statistical analytical tools to look for trends and patterns in the data. This can be done using software such as Excel or SPSS.

Another method is to use qualitative analysis to interpret the data. This entails digging deeper into the data and attempting to understand the meanings and implications of what is said.

Understanding who your users are and how they interact with your resource or service is essential to creating an effective user experience. Segmenting users provides valuable insights into user behaviors, helping you better identify, target, and respond to their needs. Empathy maps, journey maps, affinity diagrams, and user personas all offer powerful yet simple solutions for gathering contextual data about who your users are and what their preferences may be. This may be time-consuming, but it is imperative to gain a 360-degree view of your user base, which will result in lasting relationships built on trust.

Organize the Data into Groups

Organizing data from market research can be tricky, depending on the size and scope of the project. There are a few different ways to group data from market research. One way is to group it by demographics, such as age, gender, income, etc. Another way to group data is by user segments, such as students, faculty, or community members. Additionally, data can be grouped by resource category, type of service used, or any other number of factors. Ultimately, the best way to group the data will depend on the specific research goals and objectives.

However, there are a few general tips that can help make the process go more smoothly. First, it is important to decide what groups or categories you want to create. This will depend on the specific research you are doing and the goals of your project. One way to organize data is to create a spreadsheet or table with the different groups as columns. This can be helpful in visualizing the data and making sure all of the information is accounted for.

Another option is to create digital folders or files for each group, which can be helpful if you have a lot of data or if you need to access the data frequently. For example, you could have a group for demographic data (age, gender, income, etc.), a group for psychographic data (lifestyle, personality, values, etc.), and a group for behavioral data purchase history, media consumption, etc.). Another way to group your data is by the source of the data. For example, you could group it by primary data, which would be data that is collected firsthand, such as through surveys, interviews, and observations, and group it by secondary data, which would be data that is collected from sources that already exist, such as census data, government data, data from previous studies, or data that you purchased from a research firm. You could also group your data by the time period in which it was collected. For example, you could have a group for the data you collected last month, a group for the data you collected last year, and a group for the data you collected five years ago.

Addressing Equity for All Users

Market research can help identify user needs and preferences and potential areas of inequality. It can also help assess the effectiveness of current equity-related policies, marketing campaigns, and outreach programs. By understanding the landscape of user needs and wants, we can develop targeted interventions that are more likely to be successful in promoting equity. This is especially important when designing resources or services that will be used by a wide range of people, as it ensures that no one is being left out or disadvantaged. This includes considering any potential barriers to equity that may exist.

Market research can help develop strategies to address any issues of inequity. For example, suppose market research indicates that a particular group of users is not using a resource or service due to a perceived lack of equity. In that case, the library can take steps to address that issue, which can lead to increased visits and user satisfaction. There is no "one-size-fits-all" answer to addressing equity for all users, as the needs of each user group will vary depending on their specific circumstances. However, some general principles include the following:

- Ensure that all users have access to the same essential features and functionality, regardless of their individual abilities or limitations.
- Provide flexible options for how users can interact with the resource or service so that everyone can find an approach that works best for them.
- Offer clear and concise instructions and documentation so that users can easily understand how to use the resource or service.
- Provide user support that is responsive and helpful so that users can get assistance when they need it.

Organizing Data to Address Pain Points

Understanding user needs and pain points is an essential part of creating empathic library marketing solutions that provide value. Once you have organized the data, it's time to start addressing them. When designing solutions to the pain points, always think about how the solution will benefit the user. This includes users with disabilities, users from different cultures, and users with different needs. It is important to test these solutions with users to ensure that they are effective. Finally, you need to constantly monitor your users' pain points and adjust solutions as needed.

There are a few key things to keep in mind when conducting market research to address pain points equitably for all users. First, it's important to ensure that the research is conducted with a representative sample of the target market. This means that the sample size should be large enough to accurately reflect the demographics of the target market and that the research methods used are effective in reaching the target market. Once the research is conducted, it's important to analyze the data carefully to identify any patterns or trends. This data can then be used to develop solutions that address the pain points identified. It's also important to keep in mind that what works for one group of users may not work for another, so it's important to tailor solutions to the specific needs of each group.

Conducting a Needs Assessment for Empathic Library Marketing Solutions

A needs assessment is a process that helps determine how best to meet the needs of a particular group of people. When it comes to library marketing, this means determining who your target audience is, what their needs are, and how you can best meet those needs with your library's services and resources. To do this effectively, libraries must first understand their mission—who they are serving and why—then identify potential audiences and assess their level of need for library services. Once these steps have been completed, librarians can start working on marketing solutions that are tailored specifically for their target audiences. A needs assessment is an invaluable tool that helps library marketers, and librarians identify the user needs and pain points that can be addressed through library marketing initiatives. Let's discuss the steps involved in conducting a successful needs assessment.

Step 1: Identify Your Target Audience

This first step involves researching current users of the library and potential new users who could benefit from its services. This research should include gathering demographic information, such as age, gender, education level, ethnicity, etc., as well as psychographic information, such as interests or lifestyle choices. The more you understand your target audience's values, beliefs, and preferences, the better able you will be to meet their needs through your library marketing solutions.

Step 2: Gather Data

Once you have identified your target audience, gather data about their needs and pain points through surveys or interviews with current and potential users of the library. You can also analyze usage data from existing users or look at reviews of similar libraries or services online to get an idea of what people are looking for in terms of services from a library like yours. Additionally, you can use social media analytics tools to monitor conversations about libraries online and see what topics come up most often when people are talking about them.

Step 3: Analyze Your Data

After collecting data on user needs and pain points through surveys or interviews with current and potential users of the library (or other methods), it's time to analyze the data to gain insights into how best to address those needs and pain points through your marketing initiatives. This involves organizing the data into categories or groups (such as "accessibility" or "user service") so that you can prioritize which areas require improvement first based on feedback received from users or potential users. It also involves looking at patterns in the data that suggest underlying issues that need to be addressed (for example, if many people mention accessibility issues when discussing their experiences at a certain library).

Step 4: Develop Solutions and Create an Action Plan

The fourth step is to develop solutions based on what you learned during the assessment process. Don't forget to use the data to create meaningful stories. You want to be able to tell a compelling story about your user and their journey. This will help you better understand the user and their needs, and it will give you a better foundation for making decisions and executing successful marketing strategies. Once you have the data, you can use it to create a prototype for your target audience. This prototype should show what the marketing goals are, and it should be made to fit the needs of the end user. It should also be designed in a way that reflects the values and goals of the library. The prototype will serve as a guide for further development and will help you make sure that you are creating the best possible solution for the target audience. This prototype can then be tested with users to ensure that it meets their needs.

Once again, make sure that all stakeholders are included in this process. It's important that everyone has input on how the solutions should be implemented so that there's buy-in from all sides. After this step is complete, create an action plan outlining how each solution will be implemented over time so that there are clear expectations for everyone involved in the project.

A successful needs assessment requires careful planning and analysis of user feedback. By taking the necessary steps outlined above—identifying your target audience, gathering data on their needs and pain points, and analyzing that data—, you can gain valuable insights into how best to market your library's services so that they meet user expectations and provide solutions for common issues faced by members of your community. With this knowledge in hand, you will be well-positioned to create effective library marketing solutions tailored specifically to your target audience's needs. When you conduct a needs assessment, you create informed strategies that keep users engaged while maximizing return on investment (ROI) on your marketing efforts.

Finding Your Target Audience

Libraries are unique among service providers in that they provide resources and services to virtually anyone. They make it their mission to accommodate all the different types of people in the community, no matter their age, income level, or other demographic factors. To accomplish this, libraries must provide an extensive range of resources, which can be a challenging but also rewarding prospect. Whether the user is a student, researcher, or just a curious onlooker, there's something for everyone in libraries—although each library may have its own target audience, there is no universal target audience for them as a whole.

To figure out who a library's target audience is, it's important to see how important it is to serve everyone in the community. To do this, you need a wide range of services and materials that are interesting and meet both general and specific needs. Public libraries attract diverse users with their open-access policies, while academic libraries are generally geared toward serving students, faculty, and staff. No matter which type of library you're considering, the key is to recognize that no one type of user should dominate the landscape; instead, it's important to focus on creating a friendly environment that embraces all different types of users, from children reading stories to researchers exploring unique topics. By knowing who the target audience is and what they want from a library visit, any library can create a welcoming space where people can find what they need.

The Takeaway: Reflection and Analysis

For empathy-based design to work, we must always think about the information we've gathered to meet those needs. These patterns can help you figure out what users want and then come up with ways to give it to them. If you don't know who your audience is, you can't create content and messages that will connect with them. However, identifying your users is not always straightforward. It requires active listening, careful observation, and lots of experimentation. By collecting information about your users, you can make sure that your marketing plans and campaigns meet their needs. By knowing your target audience, you can create content that resonates with them and gets them excited about your brand. You need to know who they are, what they want, what their pain points are, how they think, how they behave, etc. So, start by asking yourself these questions:

- What are the main reasons people come to your library?
- What do they need?
- What problems do they want your library to solve?

Then, search for these qualities in your library's current marketing efforts. If there are none, start brainstorming ways you can incorporate these qualities into your next campaign. It also means going beyond the numbers and demographics to get a real sense of who your users are as people.

- What are their interests?
- What motivates them?
- What challenges do they face in their lives?

CHAPTER 7

Brainstorming or Ideating Solutions

"If you only have a hammer, you tend to see every problem as a nail." – Abraham Maslow

Figure 7. The fourth step in the empathic design process is to brainstorm or ideate solutions.

You sit at your desk and look at the latest statistics about how often people use the library. The numbers are up compared to last year, and you know that you and your team have worked hard to make the library a more welcoming and accommodating place. People of all ages and backgrounds have been coming in increasing numbers, and you can't help but feel proud. It's been a long journey to get to this point. When you first started working at the library, usage was declining steadily. After many weeks of research and analysis, you and your team gathered enough information to come up with a plan to explore the issue further. You spent countless hours organizing interviews, focus groups, and surveys in order to understand why people weren't using the resources available. Going beyond just asking questions, you also took a look at the existing challenge from different perspectives by conducting ethnographic field studies and studying usage data.

After crunching all the numbers and evaluating all the feedback, you were finally able to come to an informed conclusion about what was causing people to stay away. With this newfound insight, you knew that it was time to move forward with a solution. Through empathic marketing, you were able to understand the needs of your community and make changes that addressed those needs. Today, the library is thriving as a result. However, as you consider the coming year, you realize that you'll need to keep coming up with fresh strategies for promoting the library and its services. This is where brainstorming comes in. Brainstorming can help find new ways to make the library more known and used in the community, as well as discover new ways to improve the services it already offers.

Brainstorming for Solutions

Brainstorming is an important part of any marketing campaign, and the digital age has created new opportunities for brainstorming sessions. Brainstorming is a creative process that businesspeople often use to come up with new ideas and solutions. It's a structured discussion or meeting in which participants generate ideas, share perspectives, and build on other people's ideas with the goal of finding solutions to a specific problem. The process of brainstorming has been studied for decades and is known for being highly effective when done correctly. It can be done alone, but typically, it involves a group of people getting together to talk about a challenge or problem and come up with a variety of potential solutions by approaching issues from various perspectives. Brainstorming can be an effective way to generate lots of ideas quickly, and it can help to encourage creativity and outside-the-box thinking.

Setting up Ground Rules

A few simple rules should be set up to ensure the brainstorming session goes well. First, staff should come to each session prepared with ideas in mind so that conversations don't get too off-topic. Encourage open brainstorming but set a time limit to keep conversations moving in a logical way and stop people from talking about different things. Don't forget to review the session's goals at the beginning; it will help direct thinking and produce meaningful ideas that address the research objectives. Collaboration is important, so encourage everyone on the team to take part, respect each other's opinions, and value each person's ideas. Building upon one another's ideas is encouraged so long as it respects diverging opinions. Also, criticism should be helpful and kind; personal attacks don't belong in a brainstorming session.

Refrain from deciding which ideas are good or bad until all participants have had a chance to express themselves and actively listen to others to gain a broader understanding of the issue at hand, focus on practical solutions, and generate as many ideas as possible, regardless of how "out there" they may seem. Participants shouldn't overthink the problem or try to solve it during the first brainstorming sessions. They should wait until the implementation stage to do this. Next, it's important to stay on topic and guarantee that the ideas shared are reasonable and possible. Finally, make sure each team member has a chance to contribute their own insight and become fully involved in the discussion. One useful technique is to have each person write down their ideas on individual pieces of paper, sticky notes, or in an online document before the session. This can help create a sense of ownership over the ideas and allow people to build on each other's suggestions.

Once you have collected all the ideas, you can start narrowing them down and develop a plan of action.

One way to generate fresh ideas is to hold digital brainstorming sessions online. With digital tools, you can connect with users from all over and get feedback in real-time. You can invite users from all over the community to participate, and you'll be surprised at the wealth of creativity and ingenuity they bring to the table. Using online brainstorming tools like Miro, Mural, Google Whiteboard, Microsoft Whiteboard, Zoom Whiteboard, or Stormboard can help you gather input from team members in different departments or working remotely. Most brainstorming tools can also be used anonymously, allowing for a more diverse range of ideas and perspectives.

Creative Brainstorming Strategies

Now that we've established that brainstorming is an essential tool for problem-solving, idea generation, and innovative thinking and that it can serve as a powerful source for building and expanding on ideas, creative brainstorming techniques can help you open your imagination, come up with new ideas, and improve your ability to solve problems. Brainstorming, as a type of problem-solving activity, is a collaborative approach to generate ideas, explore different options, and build consensus. When you brainstorm, you're not expected to have the answers or solutions immediately. The best results often come after the session when you have time to reflect on the ideas generated. Brainstorming also has many benefits. It can spark creativity, help you work through challenges, improve decision-making skills, build collaboration, and increase receptivity. Group brainstorming sessions can help you develop ideas, solve problems, and create solutions in less time, with less effort, and with higher quality and results than when you work alone.

While most brainstorming techniques focus on ideation and idea generation, not every one is equal. The following strategies are proven to boost the effectiveness of your brainstorming sessions and help you develop more ideas. Whether you're working in a team or looking for a solo solution, you can combine the following techniques or develop your own to generate more ideas and unique solutions and solve problems faster. Although not exhaustive, these are some creative brainstorming techniques that I find useful, and that can help you get the most out of your problem-solving sessions:

- brainwriting
- SWOT or PESTLE analyses
- start/stop/continue
- mind mapping
- reverse brainstorming
- brainstorming games
- random word association
- word clouds
- design thinking
- the Six Thinking Hats
- the Delphi technique
- Abraham Maslow's Hierarchy of Needs

Brainwriting

Brainwriting is a brainstorming technique that helps you generate ideas with speed and structure. It's a group process in which all participants write down their ideas on a single sheet of paper. These ideas are then shared and discussed with the group, and a new sheet of paper is created for the next round. Brainwriting is especially useful for groups that aren't very creative, and it can be done in a short, structured way that helps everyone focus on the task at hand. This technique is best used when you have a specific goal, such as developing new marketing strategies or resource ideas.

SWOT and PESTLE Analyses

The SWOT analysis framework is another useful tool for library marketers. This framework helps identify strengths, weaknesses, opportunities, and threats associated with any project or initiative. It can help librarians identify potential issues before they arise and uncover new opportunities for growth and development. SWOT stands for strengths, weaknesses, opportunities, and threats and is a form of strategic brainstorming and planning focused on understanding how internal factors (strengths and weaknesses) interact with external elements (opportunities and threats). Another useful tool is the PESTLE analysis (political, legal, economic, social, technological, and environmental), which looks at a wider range of external factors than the SWOT analysis.

Start/Stop/Continue

Start/stop/continue is a popular exercise for groups of all sizes because it helps to quickly get to the heart of what works and what doesn't. It can be used to assess team performance, project management, marketing strategies, or any situation where progress is made. The concept involves asking participants to identify something they would "start doing" in the future, something that needs to "stop being done," and actions that should "continue being done." This simple structure is a great way for you to make sense of successes and challenges, dive into areas of improvement, and formulate clear strategies for the future.

One example would be initial discussions about what library marketing goals can be achieved. Some initiatives that need to be started could include the creation of partnerships with local organizations or businesses, establishing a customer service program, and advertising the library's services on social media platforms such as Facebook and Twitter. Those practices that should be stopped might include outdated methods, such as printed flyers (unless absolutely necessary) or attending one-time health and wellness fairs. Finally, initiatives deemed successful in reaching audiences should continue, such as creating a website, developing interactive content, and running meaningful ongoing programs.

Mind Mapping

Mind mapping is a brainstorming technique that helps you generate new ideas and solve problems by mapping out your thoughts in a visual way. In this brainstorming technique, you use different color-coded images, words, and symbols to visually organize your ideas, thoughts, and perspectives in a single document. This allows you to see your ideas and perspectives in a new way and combine them with different thoughts and perspectives to create new insights and generate ideas. Mind mapping is a great technique for solo brainstorming, especially if you want to combine visuals with words to come up with creative ideas and solutions. To create a mind map, start with a central idea and then branch out from there, adding ideas and information as you go.

Reverse Brainstorming

Reverse brainstorming is a creative method for coming up with ideas that start with the end result. This means that instead of thinking about the problem, issue, or goal that you need to solve or come up with ideas for, you think about the solution or outcome you want to achieve. You start with the final outcome, idea, or solution and then work backward to the present situation, problem, or issue you're trying to solve. Reverse brainstorming is especially useful for creative problem-solving, and it can help you come up with more ideas, generate unique solutions, and solve challenging problems faster.

Brainstorming Games

If you're looking to break the ice in a group setting and come up with more ideas quickly, brainstorming games can help you do both. Brainstorming games are fun, creative activities that can be used during group brainstorming sessions to help everyone get more creative and generate more ideas. They can be used as part of your group ideation process or even incorporated as part of a creative teambuilding event. There are many games you can use during a brainstorming session to help you come up with more ideas more quickly. Following are a few of the most popular brainstorming games you can use.

The dictionary game is a great introductory game for first-time brainstormers. This game starts by having everyone in the group pick two words from a dictionary that they find interesting. Then, each person takes turns presenting their chosen words and explaining why they chose them and how they relate to each other. After everyone has presented their words, the group discusses potential ideas based on those words. This game helps jumpstart creativity because it allows everyone to think outside the box and create something new from two seemingly unrelated words.

The card game requires at least three people (though more is better). It begins by giving each person five random cards from a deck of playing cards or flashcards with various objects on them (e.g., animals, fruits). Everyone takes turns laying down one card at a time while discussing what potential ideas each card could represent or how they could be combined into something new. This game encourages collaboration as participants must work together to come up with creative solutions and build on each other's ideas.

The pattern game is perfect for groups that are comfortable working together since it requires players to identify patterns between objects or ideas before coming up with different ways those patterns could be used. To play this game, start by laying out several objects (or pictures representing objects) on the table in front of the group or drawing them on a whiteboard or chalkboard if available. Have everyone look at the items one at a time and see if there are any patterns. Then, suggest ways these patterns could be used in different situations or with different resources. This game helps boost critical thinking skills and encourages collaboration.

The retreat game is best suited for larger teams that need to work together on bigger projects, as it requires participants to step away from their computers and meet face-to-face to come up with new ideas or solutions for problems they may be facing. During this "retreat," participants should try their best not to use technology (i.e., no laptops!) so that they can focus solely on using their creativity rather than relying too heavily on technology or research material available online, which may hinder their ability to think outside-the-box when coming up with solutions, ideas, resources, etc.

The thought-virus game is great for larger groups looking for an interactive way to engage with each other while generating new ideas and solutions. To start playing this game, have everyone write down one idea related to whatever topic you are brainstorming about, then pass it around until all participants have added something to it before passing it back around again until a completely new idea has been generated from just one seed thought! This ensures that all voices are heard, encourages collaboration among team members, and stimulates creative problem-solving skills.

RANDOM WORD ASSOCIATION

Random word association is a type of brainstorming that helps people develop new ideas and get out of their mental ruts. It's a group process in which participants are given a random word and then asked to think of associations and connections with that word. These associations can then be used to develop creative ideas, find new perspectives, and generate new solutions to problems. This is a simple brainstorming exercise that can be done in a group setting in a short time and can help you generate many ideas quickly.

WORD CLOUDS

A word cloud is a visual representation of the most common words or themes used in a group discussion or brainstorming session. You can make a word cloud by hand with Sticky notes or use an online word cloud generator. You can use this visual representation to identify common themes in your brainstorming session and determine the ideas and perspectives that are most common among the group. Word clouds are especially useful in group brainstorming sessions where you want to capture ideas and insights without using a physical medium. They can be used to visualize your brainstorming session and help you identify common themes and ideas quickly.

Design Thinking

Many libraries are looking for creative ways to market their services and increase engagement with their users. Design thinking is a method that many organizations use to find new ways to solve difficult problems. It was created by the Stanford Research Institute. IDEO then took it and made it into a design process for coming up with creative ways to solve problems. Design thinking is a process that is very flexible and can be used to come up with new ideas, solve problems, and create new resources or services, among other things. When using design thinking, you break down your goals into smaller steps, making sure that you are always working toward your goals. You can then use different tools to help you stay on track and keep moving toward your goal.

Design thinking is a great way to get library users involved in marketing solutions that fit their unique needs and preferences. The five main steps of the design thinking process are getting feedback from the user, testing assumptions, coming up with ideas for solutions, making prototypes, and testing them with the user. Gathering input from library users at the beginning of the process lets librarians better understand their wants, needs, and pain points when it comes to marketing services or resources. Exploring assumptions lets library marketers look at common themes among library users about different topics in an unbiased way. Brainstorming or mind mapping is the first step in developing solution ideas. Building prototypes of solutions helps get rid of bias by giving library users a real resource or service they can try out before putting a lot of time into making a solution that might not meet their needs. Finally, testing these prototypes allows them to see firsthand how they feel about the idea and what modifications should be made before implementing it as a solution.

Six Thinking Hats

Developed by Dr. Edward de Bono, the "six thinking hats" technique is designed to help individuals and groups think more creatively and effectively. Each group member is assigned a different color hat, corresponding to a different type of thinking: yellow for optimism, blue for thinking, white for factfinding, green for creativity and potential solutions, black for criticism, and red for emotions. By utilizing the different colored hats, everyone can bring their insights and opinions to the discussion. This can help generate fresh ideas and find new ways of looking at old problems, ultimately leading to more efficient decision-making processes. Not only does this promote more holistic problem-solving by introducing a variety of approaches, but it also breaks down tasks for a more effective workflow structure, allowing teams to work collaboratively and independently.

- Yellow hat thinkers should strive to uncover the benefits and positives in the solutions proposed by their collaborators.

- Blue-hat thinkers are expected to take a step back and view the big picture, provide an overarching perspective on the problem, and objectively evaluate its efficacy. This thinker is looking for ways to structure and organize the problem-solving process.
- White hat thinkers are supposed to assess the facts of the situation and make sure that all relevant data is considered before coming up with a solution.
- Green hat thinkers are encouraged to think "outside the box" and come up with creative and innovative solutions.
- Black hat thinkers are responsible for exposing potential risks and vulnerabilities in the proposed solutions so that teams can address these issues before implementing their ideas.
- Red hat thinkers are encouraged to express their feelings, hunches, and intuitive reactions to a problem without worrying about the evidence or logic behind them.

The Delphi Technique

The Delphi Technique is a creative technique that can be used to generate ideas, solve problems, and come up with new solutions. The Delphi Technique involves giving people a problem or challenge and then asking them to write down anonymous answers, which the group leader collects and shares with everyone. The group's ideas are then brought back to the group for more discussion and improvement. This could lead to more varied and valuable results than traditional brainstorming methods. This method also lets the group learn from the knowledge of both experienced and less experienced members without any one person's bias getting in the way. Each person's opinion is given the same weight. It is a valuable way to solve problems because you can get many different points of view from the people who take part.

The Delphi Technique can be applied to both large groups and smaller teams, and it can be done in person or online—in fact, it's ideal for groups whose members are geographically separated. It takes time and effort to come up with the perfect solution, but large organizations frequently use it, and when done correctly, it can also be effective for smaller teams.

The Delphi Technique is a valuable tool used to reach consensus in groups. It combines the collective opinion of individuals while protecting each person's anonymity. The fact that the technique is anonymous also lets people talk honestly about sensitive issues or topics. Through multiple rounds of anonymous or open dialogue, everyone can freely share their ideas and thoughts without worrying about being judged or criticized. It starts with naming and identifying a problem and then asking people in the group to develop possible solutions. The solutions are then sent out in an anonymous questionnaire, where individuals are asked questions about their solution (this can be done before the meeting via email survey). After the information is gathered and reviewed, the solutions are tweaked until everyone can agree on one answer.

To ensure that all involved parties understand what it takes to deliver such results in a timely fashion, this technique should preferably be executed during either a one-day retreat, two separate meetings, or via email. This helps ensure that all members have had their input heard and considered. In the end, this collaborative approach gets the best results and helps members get along better so they can work better together, especially in times of crisis. It's a group process that can be done in person, online, or using a combination of the two and relies on the core principle of anonymity.

Kaufman's Problem-solving Model

Kaufman's Problem-solving Model is a five-step process designed to help identify and solve problems in an organized and methodical manner. The five steps are as follows: (1) identify or define the problem, (2) gather information or data, (3) generate possible solutions by analyzing the data, (4) select an option, and (5) make decisions or implement the solution. By following these steps, you can ensure that you have identified all relevant factors when coming up with a solution. Once a needs assessment has been completed, it's time for library marketers to use Kaufman's Problem-solving Model to develop creative solutions for addressing those identified needs. When defining the problem, it's important for marketers to thoroughly research potential solutions before deciding on one so that they can make sure it fits with the library's mission and goals. During data collection, marketers need to collect as much data as possible so that they have enough information when making decisions or implementing solutions. Finally, when analyzing data and making decisions or implementing solutions, it is important for marketers to consider all angles before settling on one solution to ensure that it is both effective and cost-efficient.

Abraham Maslow's Hierarchy of Needs

Abraham Maslow's Hierarchy of Needs is a psychological theory that explains how people prioritize their needs and wants. The hierarchy of needs can be used in brainstorming by letting people base their ideas on the needs that must be met for them to come up with useful solutions. Maslow's Hierarchy of Needs is an idea that shows how people usually take care of their needs. It shows that, when given a choice between two needs, people will satisfy the one that is lower on their priority list first before moving on to the next need. According to Maslow's Hierarchy, people have five basic needs: physiological, safety, love/belonging, esteem, and self-actualization.

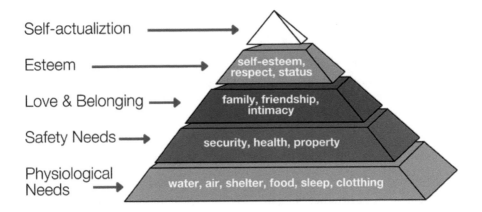

Figure 8. Maslow's Hierarchy of Needs illustrates how people generally satisfy their needs in order of importance from the bottom up.

These five needs are arranged in a pyramid, with the most basic needs at the bottom and the most advanced needs at the top. As people work their way up the pyramid, they prioritize their needs in order of importance. At the bottom of the pyramid are the basic physiological needs such as food, water, and shelter. These are the most essential needs that must be met for people to survive. Next comes safety, which includes physical safety, financial security, and health. Love and belonging are the third need and include the need for friends, family, and intimate relationships. The fourth need is esteem, or the need for respect, recognition, and success. Lastly, at the top of the pyramid is self-actualization, or the need to reach one's full potential.

To address Maslow's Hierarchy of Needs in marketing solutions for library users, split the team into five separate groups. Each group would focus on one of the needs, from the most basic to the most important: physiological, safety and security, belonging and love, esteem, and self-actualization. Each group could brainstorm different ways that the library might address these needs while also meeting the goal of marketing its services to users. By focusing on one level of the hierarchy, each person can get a more complete picture of how the library can help their users and meet their different needs. Using this model will help you market your services better by not only providing information resources but also helping users reach their goals at all levels of Maslow's Hierarchy of Needs.

BRAINSTORMING WITH THE "PHYSIOLOGICAL" NEEDS LEVEL

At the lowest level of the hierarchy of needs, the physical needs level, people are looking for basic needs such as food and shelter. At this level, brainstorming participants are likely focused on the basics, such as how to construct a building or how to come up with a menu for a restaurant. The brainstorming process at the level of physical needs might be focused on brainstorming solutions to practical problems. Brainstormers might generate solutions that have immediate, concrete benefits.

BRAINSTORMING AT THE "SAFETY" NEEDS LEVEL

The next level in the hierarchy of needs is the safety needs level. At this level, people are focused on security, including financial and job stability, a sense of belonging, and health. When brainstorming at the safety level, people focus on brainstorming solutions that have long-term, concrete benefits, such as creating a better system for distributing food to people in need or coming up with ways to provide free or low-cost healthcare to people in the community. At the level of safety needs, brainstormers may be focused on brainstorming solutions that are structured, stable, and reliable. Also, these solutions are likely to be useful in a wide range of situations. Solutions at this level may be oriented toward long-term benefits.

BRAINSTORMING WITH THE "LOVE AND BELONGING" NEEDS LEVEL

People want to be a part of a group to feel connected and appreciated at the level of love and belonging they need. At this level, brainstormers are focused on brainstorming solutions that are sentimental, affectionate, and interpersonal. Solutions at this level may have immediate utility, such as coming up with a new greeting or a new farewell. At this level, solutions may have a symbolic meaning, such as creating a new mascot for a sports team. Solutions that foster a sense of belonging and positive emotions will be prioritized by those brainstorming at the love and belonging level of needs. These solutions may have a personal connection to the people involved, such as creating a gift that has sentimental value. Solutions at this level may be oriented toward short-term benefits, such as increasing goodwill between your users and your library.

BRAINSTORMING WITH THE "ESTEEM" NEEDS LEVEL

At the esteem needs level, people are focused on how they are perceived. At this level, brainstormers are looking for recognition, achievement, and respect from others. At this level, solutions may work but have no value in and of themselves. For example, coming up with a new way to organize a workplace or a new organizational chart is an example of a solution at this level. Solutions at the esteem needs level may have a personal connection for the people involved, such as creating a new award that recognizes people for their achievements. Solutions at this level may be oriented toward short-term benefits, such as boosting the morale of a team that has just lost a game.

BRAINSTORMING WITH THE "SELF-ACTUALIZATION" NEEDS LEVEL

At the highest level of the hierarchy of needs, the self-actualization needs level; people are focused on self-fulfillment and creativity. At this level, brainstormers are looking to create something meaningful and new. At this level, solutions may have no practical application, such as creating a new piece of art or a new work of literature. Solutions at this level may have a personal connection for the people involved, such as writing a new story about a person or a place that has special meaning for them. Solutions at this level may be oriented toward long-term benefits, such as coming up with a new campaign that is meaningful to a wide variety of people.

The Importance of Brainstorming to Understand the Users' Needs

Participants in a brainstorming session will be better able to come up with meaningful solutions if they understand the user's needs. The requirements that must be met for the ideas to be meaningful to the participants can serve as a foundation for their thinking. What are the user needs? How can they be met? What are their pain points? What would make their lives easier? By having a better idea of what these people need to feel satisfied, you can create a more meaningful brainstorming session and start to come up with possible solutions.

Keep in mind that there is no "one-size-fits-all" solution—what works for one library might not work for another. The key is to make sure that your solution fits the needs of the people you want to reach. In this phase, it is helpful to include all stakeholders in a discussion of the ideas that have been generated so that they can add their own thoughts and ideas. After you have a good number of ideas, you can start evaluating them to see which ones are most feasible and will have the biggest impact on your users. During this phase, it is essential not to get too caught up in details; instead, focus on generating as many ideas as possible. Ideas can't be forced. That is why brainstorming is often referred to as a "letting ideas flow" process.

The Takeaway: Brainstorming to Develop Solutions

There are a few things to keep in mind when brainstorming for solutions in empathic design. First, it is important to think about the needs and wants of your target user. What are their pain points? What do they need or want from a resource or service? Once you have a good number of viewpoints, you can start narrowing them down in the next phase. A mind map or brainstorming can help make sure that all stakeholders are considered during this process.

This way, each idea or thought is visualized in a single space and can be linked to other relevant ideas. This will allow you to see all the ideas in one place and start grouping them together. It also allows you to start making connections between different ideas that you may not have thought of before. Second, it is important to think about how your solution can address those needs and wants in a way that is both innovative and efficient. Third, you should think about how realistic your solution is. Can it be put into action with the resources you have? Finally, it is important to think about the potential impact of your solution on both the user and the larger community. Will it make their lives better? Why? Brainstorming can be a helpful tool for generating new marketing solutions, but it is just one piece of the puzzle. Implementing the solution is where the real work begins.

CHAPTER 8

Crafting Empathic Library Marketing Solutions through Prototyping and Testing

"If you want to go fast, go alone. If you want to go far, go together." – African proverb

Figure 9. The final step in the empathic design process is to create potential prototypes and test solutions.

The final step in the empathic design process is to prototype and test the solution you brainstormed, as this helps ensure that the final solution meets the users' needs and expectations. The prototypes created are tailored to fit user needs, ensuring no gap between what they want and what they receive. By taking this extra step, you improve both the experience for your customers and the effectiveness of your marketing initiatives because you can better connect with them.

With customer satisfaction being key to success, having empathy should be an integral part of any design process. Prototyping is an important part of the empathic design process because it helps designers learn more about their users and how they use products. Additionally, by creating prototypes based on user feedback and research, libraries can ensure that their services and programs are up-to-date and relevant. Developing prototypes with user empathy and understanding is a great way to create experiences that exceed expectations.

Empathy involves not just understanding but caring about the needs of customers. When libraries know this much about their users and what they want, it's easier for them to develop marketing plans that meet the needs of their audiences. Effective marketing is rooted in empathy for users and a desire to ensure product use results in positive satisfaction. Library marketers don't have to worry about insufficient tools, channels, campaigns, or strategies. However, it's important to remember that each has its own unique purpose, which must be considered when developing a library marketing solution. Goals should always be clear so that effective campaigns can reach the right people and work toward a bigger goal.

Also, once you've set the goal and campaign details, developing the right tactics and strategies is important because they directly affect your ability to reach the goals. Keeping an eye on your competition and other departments can also provide insight into which solutions work best in a given market. This chapter will discuss library marketing solutions, from planning and strategizing to implementing and testing them. We'll explore the difference between library marketing solutions, channels, campaigns, goals, and strategies. In addition, we'll discuss the importance of gathering user insights to create tailored solutions based on their wants, needs, patterns of behavior, and motivations. Finally, we'll explain how personalization can help libraries form a deeper connection with their audience.

Library Marketing Solutions (Ideas, Tactics, and Strategies)

Getting the word out about library services and resources can be hard, but there are several effective ways to do so. Libraries have many ways to reach out and keep patrons updated on their services, resources, and programs. While flyers and newspaper ads are some of the more traditional methods, web or social media campaigns can be more effective in getting the word out. Here are five library marketing solutions that libraries can use to communicate about their services, programs, and resources:

- Social media campaigns. Libraries can use social media to send targeted messages to users and share interesting content quickly and easily.
- Online advertising (ads). Libraries can use online advertising platforms such as Google Ads and Facebook Ads to reach their target audience and to reach a wider audience that may not be familiar with their offerings.

- Email campaigns help keep current library users up to date on changes to services or new programs to stay in touch with their users and promote their services and resources.
- Events. Libraries can put on events to get people involved and spread the word about their services and materials. Events and programs are a great way to build relationships with local community members.
- Content marketing, such as blog posts or videos, helps libraries educate people on library resources and interesting, informative content while also boosting visibility.

Each of these methods has its own advantages, so libraries can choose the ones that make the most sense for their individual needs and budgets. In the end, the best results will most likely come from using a mix of these methods to reach more people.

The Differences Between Library Marketing Solutions, Channels, Campaigns, Goals, and Strategies

Libraries must inform their users about the wide range of services, collections, events, and classes available in the library and online. At the heart of each successful library marketing effort lies the difference between a library marketing solution, channel, campaign, goal, and strategy. Library marketing involves connecting these elements with potential users. This is done through solutions that include communication channels such as printed posters and newsletters, social media, and other digital marketing campaigns. Some libraries use marketing to get more people to sign up for events or classes, while others hope to get the word out about their services or get people to visit their website or download their app. The strategies chosen by your library should reflect the resources you have available, typical budget constraints, and a careful examination of what messages their target audiences are most likely to find resonant.

As libraries grow and technology makes it easier for them to tailor their messages and reach a larger audience through more advanced solutions and campaigns, it's important to figure out how to best combine all of these parts into effective library marketing practices. A library marketing solution is an overarching plan that shows how staff, budget, and other resources will be used to coordinate messaging strategies through the right channels. *Channels* are messages sent to users through any form of communication, print or electronic. *Campaigns* focus on achieving goals while sending a certain message. *Goals* are what the library professionals want to happen, but they can also be things like getting more people to use the library or reading new books.

On the other hand, goals are specific results that are wanted after putting the strategy into action. They can evaluate how well the plan has reached its objectives. Goals should be measurable and attainable, with clearly defined timelines demonstrating tangible progress. *Strategies* guide how campaigns communicate and engage audiences and layout which channels will be used and how they'll benefit from them. A marketing strategy is a comprehensive roadmap for success over a particular period. It provides criteria for effective decision-making, guidance for tactical implications, and channels for audience communication. It is based on a detailed analysis of customer needs and demographics, market potential, product positioning, and competition—all culminating in prescriptive, actionable steps.

When used together and as a whole, these library marketing elements will help you connect with your customers on a deeper level. A well-crafted marketing strategy combined with engaging goals creates an effective combination for driving usage.

Comparing a Marketing and an Action Plan: Understanding the Distinctions

When considering how to reach library users through empathy, it is important to understand the difference between a marketing plan and an action plan. A marketing plan lays out the steps that need to be taken to promote a product, resource, or service. An action plan, on the other hand, lists the specific tasks and goals that need to be done to finish the marketing plan. A marketing plan shows how you will promote your library's services and talk to people who might use them. It could mean using old-fashioned channels like print or radio ads or new digital marketing methods like social media to get more attention online. On the other hand, an action plan shows the steps that need to be taken to implement these strategies and reach the marketing plan's goals. For example, an action plan for reaching library users through empathy might involve creating an online survey to gauge user satisfaction, forming partnerships with local schools and community organizations, and developing customer service protocols that prioritize understanding user needs.

Most of the time, a library's marketing plan will involve developing ways to promote the library and reach new users. This could mean using digital or print ads or making content that is geared toward new and current users. However, an action plan for reaching users through empathy would involve activities designed to effectively engage with existing and potential library users to create meaningful relationships. This type of plan aims for the library team to understand and empathize with their audience by getting to know them—where they live, their aspirations, and how the library can help them achieve them. In the end, libraries are in the business of building a relationship and understanding with their users, not just making a conversion.

A marketing plan is developed to get the word out about a library's services, programs, and resources so that it can reach more people and have a more significant impact. This is usually done by making promotional materials, branding campaigns, or social media posts that speak to people who might use the library. On the other hand, an action plan based on empathy asks things like, "What do our users need? What do they desire? How can we best support them?" Marketing with empathy also entails being proactive in anticipating user needs; a well-crafted action plan will consider expanding services and developing initiatives to anticipate user feedback. By addressing quantitative analytics from a marketing perspective and a qualitative approach to connecting with users, libraries can unlock greater success for their organizations. Crafting a successful marketing plan requires both an overarching strategy and achievable goals. While the two concepts can be intertwined, they are distinct. Finally, marketing and action plans are essential in assisting libraries in effectively connecting with users through empathy while achieving larger goals.

Crafting a Marketing Plan

To create a successful marketing plan for your library, it's important to define clear goals and objectives, identify the target audience, set a timeline, and develop an action plan. The action plan should include researching different communication channels and platforms, creating content tailored to each platform or channel, creating an effective promotion strategy, and using metrics like click-through rate or impressions to track progress. A well-rounded marketing plan can help libraries reach as many people as possible and use each channel fully. This could include setting up social media campaigns, writing email campaigns, running online ads, hosting events or programs, and making interesting content marketing pieces.

To get the best return on investment (ROI) and the results you want, you should adapt each of these techniques to the needs of the library and its target audience. Also, tracking how each channel is doing is important so you can change your strategy as needed. Making prototypes of each marketing channel will help ensure the efforts are consistent with the brand and engaging. Mockups, ads, graphics, and any other visuals associated with your campaign may be included. Libraries can ensure their campaigns work by following these steps and making any necessary changes over time. Once you have all these elements, you can test your campaign and see how it performs.

The Difference Between a Marketing Plan and a Strategic Marketing Plan

A marketing plan is a comprehensive document outlining specific actions and tactics to achieve marketing objectives within a given timeframe, focusing on operational details and execution of marketing efforts. Key components include target audience, market analysis, product positioning, marketing channels, advertising, budget allocation, and a timeline. A strategic marketing plan, on the other hand, is a higher-level document that aligns marketing efforts with broader strategic goals and objectives and includes multiple departments. It emphasizes long-term goals, market positioning, competitive analysis, and the big picture. A forward-thinking strategic marketing plan helps libraries adapt to changing market conditions and evolving goals. A marketing plan is more tactical, focusing on short-term actions and implementation, while a strategic marketing plan provides a strategic framework for marketing efforts.

Tips for Creating an Empathy-driven Marketing Plan

Creating an empathy-driven marketing plan is an important step in understanding your customers. Here are some tips for creating an effective empathy-driven marketing plan:

- Research your audience. Research their needs, wants, and concerns to gain insight into what they are looking for and how you can best meet their needs.
- Identify your customers' pain points. Understanding their challenges and struggles will help you create a plan that addresses their needs and resonates with them.
- Leverage social media. Social media is a great way to connect with your customers and demonstrate empathy. Use it to listen to their feedback and respond in a timely manner.
- Test and measure. Testing and measuring your marketing campaigns is essential for understanding what resonates with your customers and what doesn't. This will help you create an effective empathy-driven marketing plan.

- Analyze customer feedback. Analyzing customer feedback is a great way to gain insight into what your customers are looking for and how you can best meet their needs. Use this information to create an empathy-driven marketing plan that resonates with them.

Crafting an Action Plan for Library Marketing Solutions

This is optional and can be included in your marketing plan, but once you have launched the library marketing solution, you can create a strategic action plan for the solution to keep the project on track. This plan should outline the goals of the solution, the target audience, and how you plan to achieve those goals. It should also include a timeline of when you expect to achieve the goals. The action plan should also address how you will measure the solution's success, which will help you determine whether or not the solution meets the target audience's needs. You should make an action plan for continuous improvement for the best efficiency and results. This can range from something as basic as regular check-ins and a timeline to more formal protocols—whatever suits your goals and progress best.

Prototyping an Empathy-driven Library Marketing Solution

Prototype development is creating a resource, program, or service prototype. A prototype is a model or representation of a resource, program, or service used to test the idea and get feedback from potential users. Prototypes are often used in the early resource, program, or service development stages. They allow businesses to quickly get user feedback and make improvements before launching the resource, program, or service.

Prototype development can also be used in library marketing. By creating a library marketing campaign prototype, libraries can quickly get user feedback and make changes before the campaign is launched. Based on empathy, making good marketing prototypes for a library means knowing the users' emotional needs and what drives them. Consider what emotions motivate people and design prototypes accordingly.

Empathy-driven prototypes can lead libraries to create marketing plans that fit the needs of their users and the community around them, resulting in better service and more effective and engaging solutions.

The process of developing empathy-driven library marketing prototypes involves testing and refining. You should always test prototypes to make sure

they work and make changes based on what people say about them. Here are the steps for developing empathy-driven library marketing prototypes:
- Understand the needs and wants of your patrons.
- Create a storyboard or mockup of the library marketing solution.
- Create a prototype of the library marketing solution.
- Test the prototype with your users.
- Make changes to the prototype based on feedback.
- Finalize the prototype.

For instance, to make a successful social media campaign for your library, you need to know your target audience and what they want. Using this information, research should be done to find out which platforms will best help the library reach its goals. Once the platform(s) have been chosen, prototype content that is tailored to the target audience's interests and needs should be created. Finally, it is important to track engagement metrics and impressions, such as likes, shares, comments, and retweets, to measure success.

Prototyping online ads is another way that libraries can reach more people and promote their services to new audiences on various platforms, such as web engine ads (Google, Bing, etc.) and social media (Facebook, Instagram) ads. You can quickly set up campaigns with these services by creating mock ads tailored to specific audience demographics. Monitor progress regularly, adjust the budget accordingly, and make sure the ads are delivered to the right audience at the right time.

To prototype an email campaign, you need a complete list of people who might be interested in the library's services or upcoming events. This list can be compiled from surveys shared on social media sites, email distribution lists, email lists gathered at events and programs, or partnerships with other departments or organizations. Once you have your list, you can make mockups of customized emails with a strong call-to-action to engage users and track results with metrics like open rate and clickthrough.

Events and programs put on by your library are also good ways to keep current users interested and get to know potential new ones. When planning events and programs for a library, it's important to consider the audience, the reason for the event or program, and the available resources. They should be planned with specific goals in mind, like giving people access to information or getting customer feedback about your institution's services. Depending on your budget, it may also be a good idea to look for partnerships or sponsorships in your community that will help you reach your goals for hosting these activities or programs. Consider who the target audience is and what kind of event or program would be most effective at engaging them. Also, consider any budget and time constraints. Once these things are clear, make a prototype that shows the main ideas of the event or program you want to plan. This can be done by creating mockups of potential branding elements, writing sample messages or scripts, developing visuals, conducting user testing, and more. The prototype should be flexible enough to allow for revisions as feedback is gathered.

Content marketing allows libraries to reach out to people for a long time because it creates long-term awareness instead of the short-term exposure that other forms of marketing (like social media posts) create. Whether you're making blog posts, podcasts, or videos, your content should be about important things to your target audience. This will help you reach people interested in similar topics or lifestyle information related to the advertised library services. When prototyping content marketing for a library, it's important to consider the target audience and what interests them, the content's purpose, and the available resources.

Start by researching what type of content resonates best with your audience. This can be done through surveys or focus groups or by looking at existing data that reveals what types of stories perform well in similar contexts. Then, build a prototype that embodies the fundamental concepts of your desired content. You should consider using other distribution channels, like newsletters, influencers, and others, to make your marketing solutions more visible and get the most out of them.

Combining these methods with what you're already doing can make an effective marketing plan that uses several channels while staying within your budget. Also, taking advantage of these options helps libraries remain connected with the community members who may benefit most from their services and ultimately drives up usage ratings, community involvement, and satisfaction.

Testing the Effectiveness of a Library Marketing Prototype

Once you have developed the prototype, it is crucial to analyze its effectiveness. The continuous improvement process of regularly measuring, analyzing, and improving your prototype is the most effective way to do this, as it helps identify areas for improvement and ensure that your library marketing solution meets user needs. In this process, users are asked to test the prototype and provide feedback. By monitoring this data and adjusting the prototype accordingly, you create a continuous improvement cycle, allowing you to incrementally move closer and closer to an optimal library marketing solution quickly and efficiently. Using continuous improvement methods like iterative prototyping can help speed up the development of these solutions and ensure they work when they are put into place.

In this last step, everyone needs to be involved to make sure that the marketing solutions are realistic and meet everyone's needs. Developing a viable marketing solution is no small task. Before putting your plans into action, it is recommended to test them with the target market or focus group that was used in the earlier steps to get their feedback. Such data helps identify any potential problems in the prototype, which can then be removed by making changes to the prototype. Following this iterative cycle of testing, analyzing, and improving can truly make for a successful library marketing solution.

Tools and Techniques for Continuous Improvement in Prototyping

There are a variety of tools and techniques that can be used to improve the effectiveness of a prototyping process. These include the following:

- **Process mapping** is a visual representation of a process that can help teams identify areas of improvement and make necessary adjustments.
- **Analytical tools**, such as data analysis software, can be used by teams to analyze data and quickly identify areas of inefficiency.
- **Design thinking** is a process of problem-solving that focuses on finding creative solutions to complex problems and making necessary changes to the process.
- **Benchmarking** is a process of comparing the performance of a process against industry standards to identify areas in need of improvement and ensure process effectiveness.
- **Lean methodology** is a process of improving efficiency and effectiveness by eliminating waste and streamlining processes.

Using these tools can help identify areas of improvement, streamline processes, improve accuracy, improve collaboration, and identify opportunities for innovation.

Managing Continuous Improvement in Prototyping

Continuous improvement in prototyping can be a complex process. Here are some strategies for managing continuous improvement in prototyping to ensure effectiveness:

- Set clear goals for your team to ensure they focus on the right areas.

- Define metrics to measure the success of your continuous improvement process.
- Leverage data, which is essential for any successful continuous improvement process.
- Focus on collaboration among your team.
- Reward success to ensure that teams are motivated to continue to improve.

Measuring the success of your library's marketing solutions in meeting the needs of your patrons can be challenging. The best way to begin incorporating testing strategies into your marketing solution or approach is to establish measurable quantitative objectives, such as increased membership numbers or increased participation in library programs and events. This data will provide valuable insights into how effective your current library marketing tactics have been, and you can then use them to finetune and optimize future campaigns for even greater returns.

When possible, try to get firsthand reports about the users through surveys or interviews, which are more qualitative than quantitative sources of information. Gathering both qualitative and quantitative feedback from your users will make sure that you have a complete picture of what's working and what isn't.

Continuous prototyping improvement can be complex, with various challenges that you or your team may face. These challenges include lack of data, limited resources, lack of collaboration among the team, limited visibility into the process, and unclear goals.

Strategies for Communicating Library Marketing Prototypes

Effective communication is key to making the most of your library marketing prototype. Reaching out to user groups, sending emails, being active on social media, and giving people incentives for sharing success stories are all excellent ways to connect with people directly. With the right approach and a continuous improvement mindset, you can tap into a larger audience that will help raise awareness of the prototype and the value it provides to your library users. Here are more possible ways to communicate your innovative library marketing prototypes and solutions:

- Contact your users directly through email, social media, and other channels and inform them about the prototype.

- Create a website showcasing the prototype and allowing patrons to interact.
- Host a focus group-style gathering—in person or virtually.
- Invite users for beta-testing and feedback sessions.
- Use print publications targeting relevant audiences.
- Network with departments, businesses, and local organizations that use your resources and services and ask them to share the prototype with their users.

The Takeaway: Using the Prototype to Launch Your Library Marketing Solution(s)

After the marketing prototype for the library has been made and tested, the next step is to put it into action or roll it out. Before rolling out the solution(s), make sure you have all the required resources. Additionally, it would be best if you had an action plan or marketing plan for the solutions. A well-crafted marketing plan should outline how to reach your customers and the tactics you will use. Set clear and realistic goals that can be monitored and adjusted as needed. Find out your customers' channels and which ones you should focus on to reach them best.

Once you have a formal or informal action plan or marketing plan, reach out to your users by creating engaging content that resonates with them. Use social media to interact with them and explore different strategies for generating leads. Work with influencers or other partners to help spread your message and reach even more potential users.

When library marketing solutions have gone through the rigorous process of prototyping and testing, the empathtic design journey has come to a successful end. Now, you have real-world examples of how library marketing strategies work. An empathetic approach to designing library marketing has enabled personalized library marketing to tap into people's feelings, values, and beliefs. It's amazing to see what comes from such careful design work in the real world.

CHAPTER 9

The FIRST Values Framework:

Putting Empathy into Action or Empathy-Centered Library Marketing Strategies

> *"People will forget what you said, people will forget what you did, but people will never forget how you made them feel."* – Maya Angelou

I was always curious about how library marketing could be done differently. I wanted to find something based on something other than the usual strategies. After much pondering, I realized a unique model was needed—one built around empathy principles. Inspired by this idea, I began forming a creative plan to develop a library marketing values thinking tool, the FIRST values framework, an acronym for fellow feeling, identification, responsiveness, self-awareness, and thoughtfulness. The FIRST values framework would allow libraries to promote their services in a way that was appreciative of their users' feelings. Libraries could use it to think about their audience to create a more meaningful connection with users. I am proud to have created a tool that will help marketers reach their goals and foster a more empathetic relationship between libraries and their users.

The First Values Framework

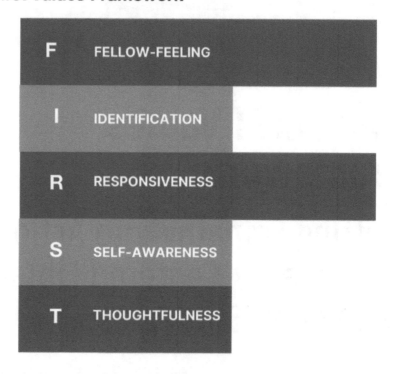

Figure 10. The FIRST values framework includes fellow feeling, identification, responsiveness, self-awareness, and thoughtfulness.

As library marketers, we are tasked with the often-difficult job of developing library marketing plans that will help draw a wide variety of library users. To do this, we must consider a range of perspectives and ideas to craft effective library marketing strategies. But how? Cultivating empathy for library users is a long-term endeavor, much like tending to a garden. It's not something that happens overnight, but with assistance from my values-based FIRST values framework, these efforts can be accelerated and become more effective in forging lasting connections between libraries and their patrons. The five core principles of the FIRST values framework provide an approach to creating empathetic messaging that resonates deeply with your community while also making sure it remains at the forefront of every step along the design and deployment process. With this thinking tool as your ally, marketing strategies no longer need to remain surface-level—they'll bloom into full stories.

Let's break down what this means.

By understanding the needs and values of your users and utilizing the FIRST values framework as a thinking tool, you can create successful results—bridging the gap between library users' needs and library services available. Putting together a marketing plan as part of a library's overall strategic plan or mission statement helps library leaders agree on the role and purpose of marketing. This sets goals and priorities, which I like to call values. Values can be thought of as the things that are important to someone based on their stage in life, their culture, and their personal experiences. Each letter in the acronym FIRST stands for a different value that can be used in any marketing plan, campaign, or solution. These values guide how the library uses marketing to get people involved and move them to act. This is because, in my opinion, marketing for a library should be seen as a tool and not as an end.

The FIRST (fellow-feeling, identification, responsiveness, self-awareness, and thoughtfulness) values framework is based on empathic design, which requires that you gain an understanding of the needs and values of the target audience, consider ideas and solutions that can meet those needs, and then integrate that design into a process that ensures empathy is used in all parts of the process. The FIRST values framework puts the user first.

The FIRST values framework puts an emphasis on empathy by encouraging library marketers to consider feelings like fellow-feeling—feeling compassion or sympathy towards people who have similar experiences or beliefs as you; identification with library values; responsiveness to criticism and feedback; self-awareness when it comes to developing campaigns; and thoughtfulness when crafting content or designing programs. For example, if your goal is to increase engagement among young adults who frequent your local public libraries, you can use the framework to help you create targeted campaigns that speak directly to them.

When it comes time to build tactics for those campaigns, you can also use the framework as a guidepost for making sure they stay true to your initial goal. The beauty of using the FIRST values framework lies in its flexibility. No matter what marketing goal or audience demographic you're trying to reach at any given moment, you can use it as a thinking tool for crafting effective messaging that resonates with your users. It also helps you be more creative by letting you look at each project from different angles and make dynamic, personalized, and flexible marketing plans for your library to meet users' needs. The FIRST values framework can be applied to library marketing to develop more customized and engaging user experiences, produce more specialized marketing materials, forge connections with users, and guarantee that empathy is infused throughout the design and marketing process. Through this framework, libraries can better serve their community by creating an environment of compassion and understanding.

The FIRST values framework can be used to guide all parts of marketing, from research and planning to execution and evaluation, and it can contribute to creating solutions that are more successful and more compassionate, meeting your users' needs in a genuine way.

By emphasizing library patrons as the primary target of marketing efforts, the FIRST values framework flips the traditional model of library promotion on its head. This shift in perspective encourages library professionals to consider library services and materials with empathy, looking at them through the lenses of fellow feeling, identification, responsiveness, self-awareness, and thoughtfulness.

Fellow-feeling

Fellow-feeling is based on empathy, understanding, and compassion for users. It involves actively listening to users, acknowledging their needs and concerns, and treating them respectfully by providing relevant experiences catering to their desires and interests. When a library embraces this attitude in its marketing efforts, it shows users that it understands their needs and values their feedback, which in turn leads to better user relationships and engagement. First and foremost, "fellow-feeling" refers to the mutual connection between a marketer and their consumer base that can be achieved through targeted outreach initiatives such as in-person visits or surveys. By doing these things, marketers can learn more about what users want from their libraries and build trust by making real connections with the people they serve.

Maya Angelou once said, "People will forget what you said, people will forget what you did, but people will never forget how you made them feel." Angelou emphasizes the importance of emotional connection in our interactions with others. This resonates deeply with "fellow feeling," or a shared sense of understanding and community. You must remember that people are not simply consumers or potential users; they are complex individuals with their own unique needs and feelings. By creating a sense of connection and community, you can build relationships that last long after the initial marketing campaign is complete.

This value of the FIRST values framework encourages libraries to put themselves in their users' shoes and understand their needs and how they would be affected by your solutions. One of the first things that people notice about a brand or company is whether they can identify with it. The hashtag #YouAreBeautiful exploded on social media in 2011 when Dove released its viral campaign showcasing a variety of women with different body types and skin tones. It was meant to connect with young women, inspire confidence in them, and help them be comfortable in their own skin. #YouAreBeautiful became the number one trending topic on Twitter. People from all over the world could identify with the message, which made them feel like they were a part of something empowering, and it struck a chord with many of those who saw the campaign because the women were relatable.

People want to feel like they are part of something, such as the company or resource that gives them that feeling. To make people feel like they are part of a community, create content that speaks to their values and goals, which leads to a more satisfying experience and a stronger bond with the library. The more you understand your users' genuine needs and the problems they face, the better you will be able to provide them with what they require and make their lives easier. We create an emotional bond with our users that is far more powerful than any marketing pitch or advertising campaign when we focus on making them feel valued and understood. And in the end, that is what will make people remember your library.

Identification

Identification is based on establishing genuine connections with users through meaningful content that resonates with their needs and interests. It encourages libraries to think creatively about how they communicate with users, engaging them in conversations explicitly tailored to their individual experiences. Users will be more loyal to a library over time if they feel more connected to its mission and services and when the library invests in building strong relationships with its users.

The value of identifying who your users are, including both regular and inactive users, and making content that speaks to your users' values and objectives is the best way to make them feel like they belong in the library. Motivations are what drive people to act and are the "why" of someone's values and desires. The "why" includes understanding their demographics, interests, and needs. By creating content that resonates with the values and motivational aspects of a person's psychology, you can foster identification and make your users feel connected to the library's resources and services. Once again, this can be done through user surveys, interviews, focus groups, or other research methods.

Identification is the process of taking on the perspectives of others—that is, it is the ability to see things from another person's point of view. While empathy and identification are closely related, they are two distinct processes. People can feel compassion for another person without necessarily taking their point of view. This is called "empathy without identification." People can identify with others without feeling empathy for them. For example, someone might identify with a political leader without empathizing with their policies. In short, empathy and identification are two separate but essential ways of understanding the experiences of others. This understanding is the first step toward finding common ground and working together toward a solution. But in library marketing, empathy can only really work if it is paired with action. Too often, we allow ourselves to feel empathetic toward our users without doing anything to help them. This type of passive empathy does nothing to improve the situation for your users. Only when you combine empathy with action can you truly make a difference. When we see ourselves in others and truly identify with their experiences, empathy can become a powerful driving force that inspires us to act on their behalf. We can create a more compassionate world by identifying with those around us.

An empathetic library marketer knows who their users are and thinks about them when developing solutions. Cultivate an interest in users by asking who they are and what they do. Another question you could ask yourself is, "How would I feel if..." It is important to remember that the user has unique circumstances and motivations that are not equivalent to yours. So, how do you identify with your users? There's no "one-size-fits-all" answer to this question, as the target audience of a library will vary depending on its location and purpose. Whatever approach you take, always keep in mind that the goal is to create a library that meets the needs of its community.

Responsiveness

Responsiveness focuses on being proactive when communicating with users instead of simply reacting or responding to inquiries or complaints. Libraries should try to keep in touch with their users on a regular basis through such channels as social media, email campaigns, newsletters, surveys, and so on. This will help them stay on top of user feedback so they can act quickly when they need to.

Responsiveness is a significant value when it comes to marketing since it plays a prominent role in user satisfaction levels. Libraries should strive to ensure that their service is highly responsive both online and off; they should strive to answer any queries quickly and accurately while also providing helpful advice that meets the user's needs. If you have a "one size fits all" marketing plan and aren't responsive, then you are likely missing out on the specific needs of your diverse users. While people are looking for brands that they can identify with, they also want brands that respond to their needs and desires. Sensing that a library is responsive can make users feel like they are being heard and valued, even if they don't fully identify with everything the library does or offers.

Responsiveness can help solve problems, help users feel heard, and allow users to think that the library truly cares about their needs and desires. Can you be more intentional? Excellent and responsive user service is important. Your library should have fast response times on social media accounts as well as an up-to-date website with frequently updated content relevant to their audience's interests. Get to know your community. What are the major events and happenings in town? Which cultural institutions are popular among locals? How can you work with those institutions to promote your library? Do you show up at the places on social media where your users are? Do you go to events that reflect your diverse users and include them in library planning? What are they looking for in a library? What services or resources do they find useful? What can you do to make their experience at the library better? This means creating a marketing plan that is flexible and adaptable and creating targeted marketing campaigns that address the specific needs of different user groups.

Self-awareness

Self-awareness involves looking inward at the library's own strengths and weaknesses so it can improve its offerings for users by taking ownership of its messaging across all platforms. Libraries need to be aware of how various aspects of service delivery impact user satisfaction levels as well as what kind of marketing appeals most to its target audience(s). Knowing these things helps libraries come up with messages that are real and meet the needs of their users.

In this component, self-awareness is broken down into three parts: awareness of your library, awareness of the community around you and their motivations, and awareness of yourself as a librarian. Self-awareness involves understanding what sets your library apart from other services—this could include unique services offered only at your library or features that make it stand out from competitors—so you can effectively market it accordingly. For example, if your library provides specialized technology support for students, this would be something worth highlighting in any advertising materials or campaigns you produce. Also, self-awareness means being aware of your own biases and prejudices. When you're trying to come up with a solution, it's important to be mindful of your own biases so that you can create a solution that is fair and just for all parties involved. We all have biases and assumptions, and they can often unconsciously guide our decisions about what we think will be most appealing or valuable to our users. It's important to take the time to understand your users' needs and preferences rather than make assumptions based on your personal preferences or experiences. From a sociological point of view, marketing is inherently flawed when it comes to issues of fairness because it often assumes that what is "marketable" is also preferable or meets society's standards of what is good. You should be especially aware of how your actions might support or challenge these ideas about marketability as a measure of quality and worthiness as users of certain services or resources.

Also, self-awareness can help you figure out what the library is doing well and what could be improved—including being honest about limitations. To be self-aware is to know your library, know your community, and know yourself. Only once you have a firm understanding of all three can you begin to craft marketing campaigns and solutions that are empathic.

Answer questions like, "Who are we as a library? What are our strengths and weaknesses? What do the library's values actually mean in relation to our users?" To help with these efforts, library professionals, administrators, the governing body, and even members of the community should all be asked to answer questions like the ones above.

It is also important to understand your strengths and weaknesses as a library marketer. Are you better at social media, writing copy, or targeting a specific audience? It's not important to be an expert in all these things, but it is important to know who you are. We're often guilty of thinking that everyone should love books, research, and libraries as much as we do. But the truth is, people have different interests and needs when it comes to the library. Try to anticipate what kinds of things might be confusing or off-putting for users, and keep in mind that your users are the core audience of your marketing, not just incidental onlookers. By being self-aware, you can focus on creating strategies that make the most of your strengths and make your weaknesses irrelevant.

Thoughtfulness

When creating marketing messages for the library, thoughtfulness reflects a conscious consideration for both the external (users) and internal (staff) environments. Being thoughtful means considering things like the content's relevance to the situation, how it will be delivered, and how clear and accessible the message is to understand. It also means thinking about things like language barriers or cultural differences between staff members or users from different departments within the organization or different groups outside the organization.

The thoughtfulness component of the FIRST values framework encourages libraries to think about the long-term impact of their decisions and actions. This means that when you're trying to come up with a solution, you should think about how it would affect you if you were in the same situation as those affected by the solution. This includes considering the potential consequences of their actions and making sure those consequences are positive. It also has considered the needs of all stakeholders—not just users—when making decisions. By being thoughtful in their decision-making process, libraries will be better able to create solutions that meet the needs of all stakeholders involved.

Marketers should also be thoughtful in their strategies and campaigns, putting effort into creating content that adds value for users instead of simply focusing on material gain for themselves as marketers or librarians. Thoughtful content should contain fascinating facts and helpful advice related to its topic so that users feel informed after reading it; it should provide an enjoyable experience rather than simply trying to sell something upfront without giving anything back in return. To do this, marketers should ask themselves, "How will our strategy or campaign make users feel?" and "Will it make their experience better or worse?" By being thoughtful and taking the time to understand what users are looking for, you can create marketing that speaks.

The Takeaway: The FIRST Values Framework

The FIRST values framework is a list of empathic values that can help library marketers develop and implement effective action plans. The five values of the FIRST values framework—fellow feeling, identification, responsiveness, self-awareness, and thoughtfulness—can help libraries at every stage of creating a solution, from figuring out what users need to respond to feedback. Keep in mind that empathy is not a one-time thing—it's something you need to work on and refine constantly. Brainstorm with your colleagues, gather people outside the staff, and ask your users. Look at your marketing materials and ask yourself how well they reflect the needs and interests of your users. Are you using language that they will understand? Are you providing information that is relevant and useful to them? Creating a brand for your library—something people will remember and understand—takes time. Your marketing should not be a one-way street; it should be a dialogue that responds to the needs and concerns of your users.

Be open to feedback and criticism and be prepared to make changes based on what you learn. Always err on the side of caution and give your users too much rather than not enough. The framework starts with the question of "fellow feeling"—how well do we understand the needs and experiences of our users? Identification asks us to think about how we can get to know our users and build trusting relationships. To be responsive, you must pay attention to how our users' needs change and adapt services to meet those needs. Self-awareness reminds us to reflect on our own biases and assumptions so that we can be sure that our actions are indeed in line with our values. Finally, thoughtfulness asks us to consider our decisions' long-term impact and act with empathy for the people we serve.

The FIRST values framework can be used to help you think empathically in a variety of outreach and marketing tactics and situations. When considering a new policy at your library, for example, you can use the FIRST values framework to examine your marketing from multiple perspectives, including those of the library user, library professionals, and the larger community. The questions from the perspective of the library user are: "What do I need? What can the library do for me? What are my challenges in using the library?" The library professional's concerns are as follows: "What does the community require? What services does the library provide? How can we reach our target audience the most effectively?" Lastly, from the standpoint of the larger community, the questions are: "How is the library perceived? How can we change negative attitudes? What is the library's positive impact on the community?"

CHAPTER 10

Evaluating and Measuring Success:

Gauging the Impact of Your Library Marketing Strategies

> *"Our job is to connect to people, to interact with them in a way that leaves them better than we found them, more able to get where they'd like to go."* – Seth Godin

Once library marketers have tested and finetuned their strategies, the next step is to evaluate the solutions implemented. This process requires collecting customer feedback for analysis on three key factors: engagement, satisfaction, and loyalty. The more successful library marketing solutions should garner higher levels of engagement, satisfaction, and loyalty among library patrons, so tracking these metrics will provide a clear picture of how effective the library's marketing strategy has been. It's important for library marketers to track and evaluate customer feedback over time so that they can make changes as needed to keep improving library marketing solutions. After putting your plan into action, step back and look at how things turned out. This will help you to understand whether or not the solution was effective in solving the problem. It is also an excellent opportunity to think about what could be improved for next time. This is a key step toward making better campaigns in the future and getting the results you want.

Before you begin the evaluation, ask yourself these questions:
- What were my goals?

- What are the available resources for synthesizing the data that will be most useful in gauging success?
- What types of library services were you promoting?
- Who was your target audience?
- What channels were you using to share library solutions?

Keeping track of the answers to these questions will give you important information about how your library promotes itself and help you make your future marketing efforts more effective.

Other things to consider when evaluating your solution include:
- Did the solution solve the problem?
- What worked well?
- What could be improved?
- What would you do differently next time?

When it comes to library marketing, it's easy to get stuck in a rut and adhere to the same methods year after year. Taking a step back and looking at how you market your library can help you find ways to improve and plan more effective campaigns. However, it's important to distinguish between testing and evaluating; while testing can help determine whether specific materials or techniques resonate with target audiences, evaluating involves critically examining whether long-term objectives were met. Testing is short-term and is a part of the empathic design process, but evaluating is a long-term process. Keep these points in mind when reviewing your library marketing efforts.

How to Measure the Success of Your Library Marketing Solutions

Once your library has created, prototyped, and implemented its library marketing solutions, you need to measure its success to understand what is working and what isn't and to identify areas for improvement.

The first step in evaluating your solutions is to set goals and determine how you'll measure performance. These goals should be specific, measurable, attainable, relevant, and timely (the SMART goal model). For example, your goal may be to increase website traffic by 25 percent over the next six months or boost circulation numbers by 10 percent within one year. Once you have clearly defined goals, it will be easier to track progress toward achieving them.

Look at the data to see which channels get the most attention. Use online and social media analytics tools to track user engagement and understand how your marketing solutions are performing. Gather customer feedback from different channels, such as online surveys, customer service calls, and social media comments. Look at customer demographics, such as age, gender, location, and income level. Also, you can use A/B testing to compare alternate versions of the same solution to identify the most effective version. All of these ways of measuring will help you figure out how successful your library marketing solutions are so you can make sure that different campaigns work together to meet goals and reach a wide range of people. All of this information can help marketers get a better understanding of their customers and develop marketing solutions that are tailored to their needs.

Finally, empathy-driven evaluation encourages marketers to think outside the box and come up with creative solutions to customer problems. The easiest way to measure success is to look at user engagement and circulation numbers. This will show you if people are responding well to your marketing strategies or not. You can also look at feedback from library users through surveys and focus groups to see how well your efforts are working.

Common Metrics for Measuring Success

Website traffic is a common metric used to measure the success of library marketing campaigns. It measures how many people visit your library's website and can help you identify where people are coming from and what content they engage with.

Engagement rate is another critical metric to track. This measures how often people are engaging with your library's content. This includes likes, shares, comments, and other types of engagement. Tracking this metric will help you understand which content resonates with your target audience and which content falls flat.

Conversion rate is another important metric to track. This measures the percentage of people who take a desired action after engaging with your content. For example, if you're running a campaign to get more people to sign up for your library's newsletter, you can track the conversion rate of people who sign up after they view your content.

Leads generated is another metric to track. This measures the number of leads generated from your marketing campaigns. This metric will help you understand how effectively your campaigns drive leads and conversions.

Finally, cost per acquisition (CPA) is a key metric to track. This measures the cost of acquiring a new customer or lead through advertising. This metric will help you understand the ROI of your marketing campaigns and adjust accordingly.

Qualitative Versus Quantitative Evaluation Methods

When evaluating and measuring the success of library marketing campaigns, there are two main approaches: qualitative and quantitative. Qualitative evaluation involves gathering feedback from your target audience through surveys, interviews, focus groups, and other methods. This allows you to understand their opinions, preferences, and experiences with your library's services. Quantitative evaluation methods include tracking website traffic, engagement rate, conversion rate, generated leads, and acquisition cost. These metrics provide a more objective measure of success and allow you to understand the impact of your marketing campaigns.

Evaluating Library Marketing Effectiveness

When evaluating the effectiveness of your library marketing campaigns, it's important to focus on the campaign's goals. Identify what you want to achieve and track the metrics, like key performance indicators (KPIs), to help you understand if the campaign is meeting its goals. For example, if your goal is to increase website traffic, track website traffic metrics. It's also important to track the results over time. This will help you identify trends and patterns and adjust your marketing strategy accordingly. Finally, it's important to look at the big picture. Don't focus on the small details. Instead, look at your campaigns' overall impact and identify improvement areas.

Key Performance Indicators for Performance Assessment

KPIs for libraries help measure their performance and effectiveness in serving their communities. Using KPIs for library performance assessment is not a one-time exercise but an ongoing continuous improvement process. Libraries should regularly review and analyze their KPIs to identify areas for improvement and make data-driven decisions. After making changes based on what they learned from KPI analysis, libraries can use the same or different KPIs to assess the impact of those changes.

Using KPIs is an iterative process that allows libraries to continually refine their services and better meet the needs of their communities. Another method is benchmarking, which involves comparing the library's performance against industry standards or best practices. By benchmarking KPIs, you can identify areas where the library is underperforming or excelling compared to its peers.

This information can then be used to set improvement targets or celebrate achievements.

For example, a library may benchmark its circulation statistics against similar regional libraries to determine if they meet the expected usage levels. If they stay caught up, they can set a target to increase their circulation by a certain percentage within a specified time frame. These KPIs help assess performance, improve services, and align your efforts with their mission and the needs of their communities. Different KPIs may be more or less relevant depending on the library's specific goals and priorities. You can combine these KPIs to comprehensively evaluate their impact and make data-driven decisions for continuous improvement. Here are some KPIs that can be used to assess library performance:

- Circulation Statistics
    - Total Checkouts: The number of items (books, digital resources, DVDs, etc.) borrowed by library patrons.
    - Renewal Rate: The percentage of borrowed items that are renewed.
- Patron Usage Metrics
    - Library Visits: The number of people visiting the library
    - Library Card Registrations: The number of new library cards issued
    - Library Program Attendance: The number of people attending library events, workshops, or programs
- Digital Resource Usage
    - E-Book and eResources Downloads: The number of digital materials borrowed or accessed.
    - Database Usage: Usage statistics for online databases, journals, and research resources
- Customer Satisfaction
    - Surveys and Feedback: Collect feedback through surveys to assess user satisfaction. Measure how likely patrons recommend the library to others.
- Collection Management
    - Weeding Rate: The rate at which outdated or low-use items are removed from the collection.
    - Collection Turnover: How frequently are items in the collection replaced or updated?
- Resource Availability
    - Hold Fulfillment Rate: The percentage of holds that are successfully filled.

- - Availability of Popular Items: Assess how often high-demand items are available for patrons.
- Technology and Access
  - Public Computer Usage: Track how often public computers are used.
  - Wi-Fi Usage: Monitor the use of library Wi-Fi by patrons.
- Faculty/Staff Efficiency
  - Faculty/Staff-to-User Ratio: Assess the ratio of library staff to patrons.
  - Faculty/Staff Training and Development: Monitor staff training and development initiatives.
- Financial Sustainability
  - Library Funding vs. Budget: Evaluate the library's financial performance regarding budget allocation and actual expenditure.
- Community Engagement:
  - Partnerships and Collaborations: Measure the number and impact of partnerships with local organizations and schools.
  - Community Event Attendance: Track attendance at library-sponsored community events.
- Accessibility and Inclusivity
  - Accessibility Compliance: Ensure the library's services, facilities, and materials meet accessibility standards.
  - Inclusivity Programs: Monitor and assess programs and initiatives that promote inclusivity and diversity.
- Digital Presence
  - Website Traffic: Measure the number of visitors and user engagement on the library's website.
  - Social Media Engagement: Track likes, shares, comments, and followers on social media platforms.
- Strategic Goal Achievement
  - Progress toward Strategic Goals: Measure the library's success in achieving its long-term strategic objectives. This can be done by tracking key performance indicators (KPIs) that align with the strategic goals. These KPIs may include metrics such as increased library usage, improved customer satisfaction, and the successful implementation of new services or programs.

○ Additionally, regular evaluations and surveys can provide valuable feedback on the effectiveness of the library's strategies and help identify improvement areas.

Improving Library Marketing Results

With a few strategic changes, you can improve marketing results through more traffic or raising awareness in the community. You must set clear goals around your marketing activities and use what works within your budget and for your demographics. Utilize all avenues available to reach potential patrons, from social media to traditional flyers. By staying ahead of emerging trends and tailoring the message appropriately, you will have more success with your marketing efforts.

Set SMART Goals and/or Measurable Goals

Before you start a library marketing campaign, set measurable goals. Set your SMART (specific, measurable, achievable, relevant, and timebound) goals. In other words, your goals should be clearly defined, quantifiable, achievable, relevant to your target audience, and have a set timeframe for completion. Ask yourself a few key questions to determine if your goal is SMART.

First, is your goal specific enough? Does it focus on a particular area, such as library marketing? Is it clear and concise? Can it be easily understood? If not, consider refining your goal to make it more focused and specific. A goal should be defined in concrete terms so that it is easy to measure progress. For example, instead of saying, "I want to increase library awareness," you can say, "I want to reach one hundred new library users in the next quarter."

Next, consider whether your goal is measurable. Is there a way to track and monitor your progress? Can you easily determine if you're on track or not? If not, think about ways to quantify your goal so you can measure your success.

Third, is the goal is achievable? Is it realistic? Do you have the resources and capacity to reach the goal? If not, consider revising the goal to make it more attainable and feasible. Fourth, is the goal relevant? Does it align with your overall mission and vision? Does it help you reach your long-term objectives? If it doesn't, think about ways to make it more relevant and connected to your library marketing goals. Finally, ask if the goal is timebound. Is there an end date or deadline? Is it clear when you should expect results? If not, add a timeline to the goal to help keep you on track and accountable. Asking yourself questions like these shows a level of empathy and understanding that will help you set and reach your library marketing goals.

SETTING SMART GOALS

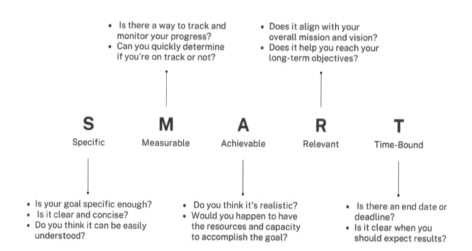

Figure 11. Setting SMART goals can keep you focused on achieving your marketing objectives.

Test and Refine

Testing and refining your library marketing strategies will significantly increase the impact of your efforts. Strive to find the best tactics for each situation, as one size does not fit all. The best approach is to experiment with a variety of options, tracking results each step of the way to identify which methods work the most effectively. Whether it's content strategy, social media outreach, or promotions, do what you can to make sure that you are getting maximum reach and long-term results from your efforts. Keeping a close eye on traffic sources and reactions can help refine future campaigns for peak efficiency and success.

Analyze Data

Analyzing the data from all marketing campaigns your library has administered can be a daunting yet essential task. Doing so, however, will offer insights into what strategies are working and which areas may need adjustments. Whether it's the effectiveness of social media posts or the response rate to email subscriptions, sorting through this data will reveal trends that will assist in refining the overall marketing plan. Identifying such correlations is integral for any successful marketing strategy, and taking time to examine this data will certainly pay off in terms of performance, ultimately bringing positive results for any library campaign going forward.

Monitor Trends

Monitoring trends in the library industry is essential for staying ahead of your competitors and creating effective marketing strategies. Trends provide insight into what other libraries in the community are doing, what types of services are in demand, and how patrons engage with library resources. It is also wise to look at national trends in library usage to get an idea of regional and local library services that may need improvement or expansion. Keeping an eye on current trends provides invaluable information that can inform marketing strategies and guide library operations decisions.

Checking ALA Connect Groups or ACRL Facebook Groups is a great way to keep up to date with current trends and conversations about library-related topics, including insight into what may be upcoming or changing within the library industry. Keeping up to date with the latest library services might also help you attract potential new customers.

Leverage Technology

One great way of reaching more people is by leveraging technology. From automated email campaigns to online advertising solutions, today's technology provides an incredible array of options that can be tailored to fit your library's budget and approach. By utilizing social media and analytics to track progress, libraries can adjust their strategies quickly and more effectively, ensuring that the most effective methods are utilized for optimum results.

The Takeaway: Gauging the Impact of Your Library Marketing Strategies

Evaluating and measuring success is essential for any library marketing campaign. It's important to keep track of metrics like website traffic, engagement rate, conversion rate, leads generated, and cost per acquisition. It's also important to use qualitative and quantitative evaluation methods, such as surveys and interviews, to get feedback from your target audience and understand their opinions on your library services. Finally, use the resulting data to identify areas for improvement and adjust your library marketing strategies accordingly. With the right strategies and tools, you can measure the success of your library marketing campaigns and get better results. By taking the steps outlined above, you will gain valuable insights into your marketing efforts, enabling you to adjust your strategy for optimum success.

Appendices

APPENDIX A: EMPATHIC LIBRARY MARKETING SOLUTIONS TOOLKIT

This toolkit includes strategies, tactics, and resources that you can use to create an empathy-driven library marketing plan. You'll find ideas for understanding the customer journey, creating an empathic library brand, and creating empathy-driven marketing strategies, campaigns, content, and tactics.

Empathic Library Brand

Developing an empathic library brand is an important part of library marketing. It requires the library to think about how its services can be more tailored to the needs of its users. To do this, the library must start by recognizing its audience and understanding their needs. It can then use this knowledge to create a welcoming, supportive brand that resonates with its users by expressing empathy. This is done by listening to feedback and adapting services to meet the changing needs of its users. In addition, the library should create a warm and inviting atmosphere that encourages people to come in and explore its offerings. This is done by offering a range of activities, events, and services tailored to the library's users.

How to Develop a Library Brand

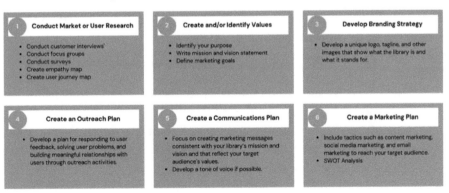

Figure 12. The six steps to developing a brand for your library.

The library should also focus on creating a sense of community. This is done through activities and events that encourage users to socialize and build relationships with each other. It is also important to ensure all library services are easy to access and use. This includes creating a library website that is easy to navigate and provides clear information on all library services.

Libraries should foster an internal culture of empathy by ensuring that library professionals are trained to be sensitive and understand patrons' needs. It also means creating a welcoming and inclusive library environment, being aware of its users' diverse needs, and striving to make its services accessible to everyone. This includes creating a library that is wheelchair accessible, providing books in multiple languages, and creating inclusive programs. Finally, the library should strive to develop relationships with its users. This is done by engaging with them on social media, responding to feedback, and offering personalized services. This will result in a library brand that is not only concerned with marketing its services but also with developing relationships with its users.

There are six steps to create a brand for your library.
- Step 1. Conduct research and collect feedback.
- Step 2. Create, refine, or revise the library mission statement.
- Step 3. Develop a library branding strategy.
- Step 4. Create an outreach plan.
- Step 5. Create a communication plan.
- Step 6. Create a marketing plan.

Let's look at each step in more detail.

Conduct Research and Collect Customer Feedback

This research should focus on understanding the needs of the library's users and what makes them unique, including their interests, motivations, and preferences. Make sure to measure the success of your library marketing branding efforts. Collect data and analyze it to understand how your target audience is responding to your library brand. This will help you adjust and finetune your library marketing strategy. Here are some tips for collecting customer feedback:
- Use surveys to gain insight into what your customers are looking for and how you can best meet those needs.
- Monitor social media to listen to your customers and respond promptly.
- Use feedback forms to gain insight into what your customers are looking for and how you can best meet those needs.

Create, Refine, or Revise the Library Mission Statement

Your mission statement should be concise, communicate the library's purpose and values, and highlight how the library will serve its patrons. The mission statement should be used as a guide for all library marketing efforts.

Develop an Empathic Brand Strategy

To ensure that your library's customers feel understood, respected, and heard, it's important to take the time to plan and execute an empathic library brand strategy.

- Take the time to survey library patrons and ask questions about their library experiences, what they want from their library, and what they think could be improved. This will give you valuable insight into how to create an empathic library brand that resonates with your target audience.
- Make sure your library's messaging and marketing materials reflect your empathic brand. Use language that conveys understanding, respect, and support. Share stories of how your library has positively impacted people's lives or how it has made their day a little bit brighter. Show your customers that you understand their needs and that you're taking action to meet them.
- Brand message and materials include making a unique logo, tagline, and other images that show what the library is all about and what it stands for. This branding strategy should be used in all the library's marketing materials, including its website, social media, and printed materials.
- Create a library atmosphere that reflects your empathic brand. Make sure your library marketing is organized to reflect your commitment to customer service. Encourage library professionals to engage with users in an empathic way. This could mean conversing with patrons about their interests, taking the time to answer questions, or offering helpful suggestions.
- Keep your users informed about upcoming events, new services, and other initiatives. Ensure your library's website, social media channels, and other marketing materials are regularly updated and feature content that reflects your empathic library brand.

Create an Outreach Plan

Your outreach plan should be about how the library will talk to its users and ensure they understand its benefits. This plan should include ways to respond to user feedback, solve user problems, and build meaningful relationships with users through outreach activities.

As academic libraries evolve, continued outreach efforts have become increasingly important. Libraries are necessary community resources, and libraries typically offer a variety of outreach programs to encourage use among all population segments. By definition, outreach is actively engaging with potential library users who may not be aware of the available resources and services. This can be done in various ways, but standard methods include promoting library events and programs, tabling at campus events, and conducting classroom presentations.

An outreach plan should start with a needs assessment, which can be conducted through surveys, focus groups, or interviews with faculty, staff, and students. Outreach efforts can be time-consuming and require a significant investment of resources, but when done correctly, they can increase awareness of and usage of the library. An effective outreach plan is essential to any academic library's marketing effort.

Once the community's needs have been identified, you can develop outreach programs and services that address those needs. For example, if a faculty member report needing more support for classroom instruction, the library could develop a program of outreach services, including workshops on using library resources for teaching. By taking a needs-based approach to outreach, academic libraries can ensure that their programs and services are responsive to the changing needs of the university community. Developing an effective outreach plan requires careful consideration of the target audience.

Consider:
- Who are you trying to reach?
- What are their needs?
- What are the best ways to reach them?

Once these questions have been answered, setting realistic goals and objectives is essential.
- What do we hope to achieve through our outreach efforts?
- How will we measure success?

Outreach plans may include special programs for specific groups, such as seniors or children, or focus on promoting awareness of library resources and services through marketing and community partnerships. Whatever the approach, developing and implementing an effective outreach plan requires careful planning and execution. A library's outreach plans are essential because they help define the library's role in the community and identify opportunities for engagement.

Communication Plan

Focus on creating library marketing messages that are consistent with your library's mission and vision and that reflect the values of your target audience.

When it comes to communicating with your library's audiences, it's important to have a plan in place. A well-written communication plan will help to ensure that your library is effectively communicating with its audiences. A library communication plan helps to ensure that your messages are clear, concise, and on-brand. It also helps to ensure that your team is on the same page and that everyone knows who is responsible for what tasks.

A communication plan is a written document that outlines how an organization will communicate with its audiences. A communication plan should be a living document that evolves as circumstances change and new opportunities arise. The plan should include the organization's goals and objectives, who will be responsible for various tasks, and what communication channels will be used. The first step in developing a communication plan is to segment the target audience. Is the library trying to reach students, faculty, or both?

Once the target audience and messages have been identified, the library can then determine the most effective channels for reaching those groups. For example, a message promoting the library's research resources would be most relevant to faculty, while a message highlighting the library's study spaces would be more appropriate for students. By developing an effective communication plan, academic libraries can ensure that their users are aware of the resources and services available to them. When developing a communication plan for libraries, consider the following:

- The mission/vision/values of the library. What is the library's mission? What does it aim to achieve?
- The target audience. Who is the library's target audience? Once the target audience has been identified, the library can then develop messages that are relevant to that audience.
- Create a communication plan:
    - Start by identifying your goals and objectives.
    - What messaging do you want to communicate and to whom?
- Identify your communication channels.
    - Will you be using social media, email, direct mail, or a combination of channels?
- Identify who will be responsible for each task.
    - Assign roles and responsibilities so that everyone knows what they need to do.

- What are the users' needs and wants?
- The resources available. What resources does the library have at its disposal? This includes both physical and human resources.
- Create a timeline for implementing your plan and setting deadlines.
- What is the budget? How much money is available to spend on the communication plan?

COMMUNICATION PLAN SECTIONS

A simplified communication plan focuses on key components that help you establish clear objectives, strategies, content, and a method for evaluating the effectiveness of your library's communication efforts and generally consists of four sections:

1. **Objectives and target audience** outline the specific communication objectives you aim to achieve, such as increasing library membership, promoting upcoming events, or improving community engagement. Be sure to make your communication objectives specific, measurable, achievable, and timebound (SMART). Also, define your primary target audience, highlighting their demographics and communication preferences. Audience identification and targeting involves understanding the primary recipients of your library's communication plan and how best to reach them.

2. **Strategies and channels:** describe the strategies you will use to reach your objectives, including the use of various communication channels. Communication channel selection determines which communication methods to use to ensure the message is spread effectively. This could include email, social media, web pages, posters, radio, etc. This section should provide an overview of how you plan to get your message across, whether it's through social media, newsletters, community events, or other means.

3. **Content and messaging** detail the types of content you will create and share in your communication efforts. Establish an effective message that resonates with the targeted audience. Include key messages aligned with your library's mission and goals. This section can also include a content calendar outlining when specific messages or campaigns will be delivered.

4. **Metrics and evaluation** will explain how you will measure the success of your communication plan. Define key performance indicators (KPIs) and explain how you will track and analyze them. Include metrics like website traffic, social media engagement, event attendance, and any

other relevant data points. Performance evaluation looks at how successful the library communication plan is and how it could be improved in the future. This includes analyzing open/clickthrough rates, engagement metrics, and user feedback.

An advanced communication plan for a library should include an executive summary, introduction and background, situational analysis, goals and objectives, target audience segmentation, key messages and value proposition, communication strategy, tactical plan, content strategy, multichannel integration, and budget and resource allocation. It should also include a detailed budget breakdown for each communication activity, KPIs), crisis communication plan, community engagement and feedback mechanisms, partnerships and collaborations, training and development for library staff, legal and compliance considerations, technology and tools, sustainability and growth strategy, and regular review and reporting.

VALUE PROPOSITION AND POSITIONING STATEMENT

A positioning statement and a value proposition are related but distinct concepts in marketing. They both play a crucial role in conveying a brand's identity and value to the target audience, but they serve different purposes:

A **positioning statement** is an internal strategic statement used to guide the overall brand or product strategy. It defines how a brand or product wants to be perceived in the market and among its competitors. It may include elements like the target audience, the market segment the brand wants to occupy, and its unique selling point. A positioning statement sets the direction for marketing efforts but may not be directly communicated to the external audience.

A **value proposition** is an external message directly communicating a resource, program, or service's unique value to its target audience. It is user-centric and focuses on the benefits, solutions, and advantages that a resource, program, or service provides to meet customers' specific needs and desires. The value proposition is often used in marketing and advertising materials to attract and engage customers. It's a concise, customer-oriented statement that answers the question, "Why should I choose this resource, program, or service ?"

In summary, a positioning statement is an internal guide that helps shape a brand's overall strategy. At the same time, a value proposition is an external-facing message that directly speaks to customers about the specific benefits and value they will receive. Both are essential in conveying a brand's identity and attracting customers, but they serve different roles in the marketing and branding process.

SOCIAL MEDIA PLAN

Now that almost everyone has a smartphone, it's no surprise that libraries are considering incorporating social media to reach out to their users. After all, social media provides an easy way for users to connect with librarians and library professionals. When developing social media plans for libraries, there are a few key things to keep in mind.

- What are your goals? Consider what goals you hope to achieve through your social media presence. Only when you clearly understand your goals can you begin to develop a plan that will help you achieve them. For example, a common goal for a library social media plan usually includes raising awareness of the library and its services, promoting events and programs, and connecting with the community. Keep these goals in mind as you develop your plan.
- Who is your audience? Before you start creating content, it's important to consider who you are trying to reach with your social media efforts. Are you looking to engage with potential library patrons who may not be aware of your services? Or are you looking to connect with current library users and promote specific events or programs? Knowing your audience will help you create content that is relevant and engaging.
- What platforms will you use? There are a variety of social media platforms out there, and it's important to choose the ones that make the most sense for your library and your audience. If you want to reach a wide audience, platforms like Facebook, Instagram, and Twitter may be good choices.
- What kind of content will you create? Once you've identified your audience and chosen your platforms, it's time to start thinking about the kind of content you want to create. Keep your audience in mind. What kind of information do they want to see? What would be most useful to them? Be sure to create content that is both informative and engaging. Will you post updates about new books and materials at the library? Will you promote upcoming events? Will you share interesting articles and resources? Planning out the kind of content you want to create ahead of time will help you stay on track and ensure that your social media efforts are effective.
- How will you monitor your efforts? Don't forget to monitor and adjust your plan as needed. Social media is always changing, so staying on top of the latest trends is important. Regularly evaluating your social media

presence ensures that you're always providing the best possible service to your community.

Social media can also promote library services and events and provide updates about changes or closures. However, it's important to remember that not all social media platforms are created equal. For example, academic libraries might want to use LinkedIn to connect with alumni or Twitter to share news and information in real-time. Ultimately, the best way to incorporate social media into your plans will depend on your library's unique needs and goals. As you look to social media to engage with users, develop and implement strategic, consistent, and sustainable plans.

To be effective, social media plans should align with the library's overall mission and goals. In addition, they should consider the needs of the library's user base and the staff members responsible for carrying out the plan. Furthermore, it is essential to clearly understand the platform or platforms on which the library will be active. Once a plan is in place, monitoring and evaluating results regularly is important to make necessary adjustments.

Social media also has several advantages. First, it is a low-cost way to reach a large audience. Second, it allows academic libraries to promote their services and events to a wider audience. Third, it allows academic librarians to engage with students in an informal setting. Developing a library social media plan can be a great way to connect with potential patrons and promote library services and events.

Social media can be time-consuming, requiring consistent posting to build an audience. Still, developing a concerted effort on social media has many potential benefits, including improved communication with patrons, increased library visibility, and enhanced marketing and outreach opportunities. However, social media can also be a time-consuming and resource-intensive endeavor. As such, it is important for libraries to carefully consider their goals and objectives before embarking on any social media initiatives. By developing a well-thought-out social media plan, academic libraries can ensure that their use of social media is strategic and impactful.

Empathy-driven Marketing Plan

Your marketing plan should focus on how the library will promote itself to its patrons. This includes developing marketing campaigns, creating marketing materials, and using digital marketing tactics. Make sure to include tactics such as content marketing, social media marketing, and email marketing to reach your target audience.

A marketing plan is a detailed roadmap that outlines your marketing strategy, tactics, goals and results over a period. Your marketing plan should start with an executive summary a brief overview of your plan highlighting the key points. Next, you'll want to include an overview, your target market analysis, and your marketing objectives. After that, you'll want to outline your marketing strategy, including your communications mix, positioning statement, and value proposition. Finally, you'll want to detail your marketing tactics, including your communication channels, promotional mix, and budget.

Here are some tips for creating an effective empathy-driven marketing plan:

- Research your audience. Research their needs, wants, and concerns to gain insight into what they are looking for and how you can best meet their needs.
- Identify your customers' pain points. Understanding their challenges and struggles will help you create a plan that addresses their needs and resonates with them.
- Leverage social media. Social media is a great way to connect with your customers and demonstrate empathy. Use it to listen to their feedback and respond in a timely manner.
- Test and measure. There are essential tasks for understanding what resonates with your customers and what doesn't. This will help you create an effective empathy-driven marketing plan.
- Analyze and evaluate user feedback. Analyzing feedback is a great way to gain insight into what your customers are looking for and how you can best meet their needs. Use this information to create an empathy-driven marketing plan that resonates with them.

Your marketing plan should cover all aspects of your marketing activities, from your overall brand strategy to specific marketing initiatives and campaigns. It should also include your target market, positioning and messaging, marketing mix, and budget. A marketing plan for libraries can vary depending on the size and budget of the library but should generally include a mix of traditional and digital marketing tools and tactics. Traditional marketing tools may include print ads, direct mail, and public relations, while digital marketing tools may include website optimization, email marketing, and social media outreach. The key is to create a mix of marketing activities that reach the library's target audience most effectively. The plan should consider the library's budget, staffing, resources, and the needs of the community it serves.

Some elements that could be included in a library marketing plan include the following:

- Develop a tagline or slogan that accurately reflects the library's mission and brand.
- Design eye-catching and informative collateral materials, such as flyers, posters, and postcards.
- Utilize social media platforms to engage with potential users.
- Create engaging and educational programs and events that highlight the library's unique offerings.
- Partner with departments and local organizations to promote the library to their users and members.
- Develop marketing campaigns around specific themes or holidays.
- Conduct market research to identify the needs and interests of the library's target audience.

Creating a comprehensive marketing plan can seem daunting, but it's important to remember that it doesn't have to be perfect. The goal is to get started and to continue to refine and adjust your plan as you go.

Here are a few tips to help you get started:

- Define your goals. What do you want to achieve with your marketing efforts? Be specific and realistic in your goals, and make sure they align with your library marketer goals.
- Research your target market. Who are your ideal users? What are their needs and wants? What are their usage habits? The more you know about your target market, the better you'll be able to reach them.
- Develop your positioning and messaging. What makes you unique? What benefits do you offer to your users? Your positioning and messaging should be clear, concise, and compelling.
- Choose your marketing mix. What marketing channels will you use to reach your target market? What type of content will you create? What other marketing initiatives will you undertake? There is no "one-size-fits-all" answer to this question, so choose the channels that will be most effective.

EMPATHIC COLLATERAL MATERIALS

Here are some tips for creating empathic collateral materials:

- Put your customers first. When creating collateral materials, focus on your customers first. Think about what they need and how you can best meet those needs.

- Use real visuals with diverse people. Use real visuals that are eye-catching with diverse people that are engaging to help your customers understand your message.
- Tell a story. Storytelling is a powerful tool to connect with your customers. Use storytelling to create an emotional connection with your customers and make your message more memorable.
- Keep it simple. Keep your collateral materials simple and easy to understand. Avoid using jargon and complex concepts that may confuse your customers.
- Use positive language. Use language that is uplifting and encourages your customers to act.
- Show your customers that you appreciate them. Use visuals and language that convey your appreciation for their library marketer.
- Use humor to connect with your customers and make your message more memorable. Use humor to make your message more engaging and lighthearted.
- Invite feedback from your customers to gain insight into what they are looking for and how you can best meet their needs.

TYPES OF COLLATERAL MATERIALS FOR EMPATHY MARKETING

Many types of collateral materials can be used for empathy-based marketing. Here are some of the most popular types of collateral materials for empathy marketing:

- Brochures. Brochures are a great way to provide valuable information to your customers. Use them to showcase your products and services in a way that resonates with your customers. Create brochures focusing on the customer's needs and how your resource, program, or service can help them. Use visuals and language that are engaging and will resonate with your customers.
- Posters. Posters can create an emotional connection with your customers. Create posters focusing on your customer's pain points and how your resource, program, or service can help them. Use visuals that are eye-catching and engaging to help your customers understand your message.
- Flyers. Flyers are an effective way to get your message out to a wide audience. Create flyers focusing on customer appreciation and how your product, resource, or service can help them. Use visuals and language to resonate with your customers and make your message more memorable.

- Email. Email is a great way to keep in touch with your customers and provide them with valuable information.
- Videos. Videos can tell stories and create an emotional connection with your customers when you share them on social media, email campaigns, and the library website. Use visuals and language to create an emotional connection with your customers and make your message more memorable.

BENEFITS OF EMPATHETIC COLLATERAL MATERIALS

Using empathetic collateral materials can help you connect with your customers and foster loyalty. Here are some of the benefits of using empathetic collateral materials:

- Increased engagement. By connecting with your customers on an emotional level, you can create a relationship of trust and loyalty.
- Improved customer experience. By understanding your customers' needs and creating materials that meet those needs, you can create a more positive customer experience.
- Increased sales. By connecting with your customers on an emotional level, you can create a relationship of trust and loyalty, which can lead to increased sales.
- Improved customer retention. By understanding your customers' needs and creating materials that meet those needs, you can create a more positive customer experience and foster loyalty.
- Improved brand awareness. Empathetic collateral materials can help improve brand awareness by creating an emotional connection with your customers. This can help you stand out from the competition and increase your visibility.

EMPATHIC BUT STRATEGIC MARKETING CAMPAIGNS

Every marketing decision should be strategic, but what does that mean? In the case of libraries, it means making decisions with the library's mission in mind. What are the goals of the library? How can marketing help to achieve those goals? It also means taking an empathic approach, understanding that each person who comes to the library has different needs and wants, which can help develop targeted marketing plans that resonate with them personally. One of the biggest challenges is figuring out where your resources are going and how to allocate them. To help you with this process, there are three major points that you should consider.

- Know what your goals are before you start. You should know exactly what you want to accomplish by launching a new library marketing campaign. If you don't have an idea in mind, it will be much easier to get frustrated during the process. So, it's important to have a clear goal in mind when starting any new marketing initiative.
- Know your audience before you start. Knowing who your target audience is can help you shape your marketing strategy and make it more effective. For example, if you know that people in your community love to read but don't visit the library as often as they should, then you might want to try some different tactics to encourage them to use the library more.
- Be realistic about how much time and money you can afford to put into new marketing initiatives. It can be daunting to imagine how much money and time you're going to need for a new library marketing campaign. But remember that there are ways to save money and do more with less (such as working with volunteers, students, interns, etc.).

ANALYZING AND REFINING THE PROTOTYPE

Developing a library marketing solution that is effective can be a daunting task. However, by using iterative prototyping and iterative thinking, you can create a solution quickly and efficiently. By following the principles of iterative prototyping and creating an action plan for the solution, you can ensure that the solution is effective and meets the needs of the target audience.

Once you have launched the library marketing solution, it is important to analyze and refine it regularly. This will help ensure that the solution is always effective and meets the needs of the target audience. Analyze the data from the tests and make changes to the prototype accordingly. Also, look for feedback from users and make changes to the prototype as needed. This will help ensure that the solution is always effective and meets the needs of the target audience.

TESTING AND ITERATION OF LIBRARY MARKETING PROTOTYPES

Once a library marketing prototype has been developed, it's important to test it and iterate on it to ensure that it meets the needs of the patrons. Testing and iteration are essential parts of the prototype development process, as they allow you to make changes to the prototype based on feedback from patrons, library professionals, and other stakeholders.

Examples of some prototype designs include empathy maps, journey maps, affinity diagramming, and user personas. Each of these prototypes presents distinct opportunities for reaching diverse target audiences and measuring results concerning promotions, engagement, and referrals. By studying how readers respond to such prototypes, libraries can create successful communications that drive participation and loyalty.

EMPATHY MAPS

Empathy mapping is a tool that helps you understand users' needs by putting yourself in their shoes helping you develop new programs and services that better meet their needs. An empathy map helps identify customer needs and expectations, motivations, and pain points and can better understand customer behavior, attitudes, and emotions. Creating an empathy map begins with four essential quadrants: think, say, feel, and do.

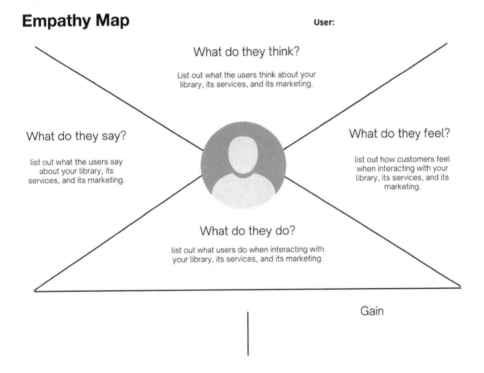

Figure 13. The empathy map.

- First, observe the user in their natural library environment. This can be accomplished through direct observation, reviewing video footage, or other data.
- Next, it is necessary to listen to the users to gain an understanding of their needs and challenges. This can be done through interviews or focus groups.
- Write down the needs and wants. Start by writing down the needs and wants of your target audience on a large piece of paper or whiteboard. Then, create four "quadrants" on the paper or whiteboard. Label each quadrant with a different motivational factor, such as—"think," "say," "do," and "feel."
    - In the "think" section, list what the users think about your library, its services, and its marketing.
    - In the "say" section, list what the users say about your library, its services, and its marketing.
    - In the "do" section, list what users do when interacting with your library, its services, and its marketing.
    - In the "feel" section, list how customers feel when interacting with your library, its services, and its marketing.

JOURNEY MAPS

Journey mapping is the process of creating a visual representation of the steps a user takes to complete a task or goal, moving customers through the stages of awareness, interest, decision, and action. By understanding each stage of the customer journey, library marketers can create tailored experiences that build trust and foster loyalty. Empathy is key to understanding the customer journey and creating meaningful connections with library patrons. This can be applied to both digital and physical experiences, and it can be used to improve user retention and satisfaction as well as identify potential areas for improvement. Journey maps can be used to identify user pain points and optimize the user experience.

Creating a customer or user journey map can provide an understanding of the customer's journey and how they engage with the library's marketing activities—it's a visual representation of the journey a customer takes when interacting with a library's marketing content. It involves mapping out the touchpoints, or points of contact, a customer has with the library, including physical and online channels.

Journey Map

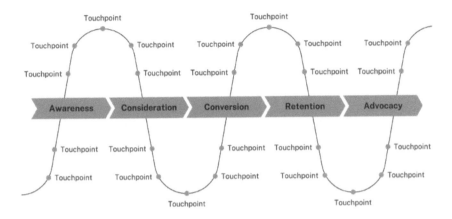

Figure 14. The user journey map.

To create a customer or user journey map, the first step is to identify the touchpoints at which they encounter the library's marketing activities. These include library websites, social media, email campaigns, and physical locations. Once the touchpoints have been identified, consider the customer's experience at each touchpoint. This could include the content they consume, their reactions and emotions, and how they interact with the library's marketing activities. This may include the initial contact, browsing the library website, researching library materials, purchasing the materials, and finally, the post-use experience. Once the various stages have been identified, the library marketing team should create a timeline outlining each stage. This timeline should include the customer's touchpoints at each stage, such as what information they are looking for, their actions, and how they feel.

Here are the steps in creating a user journey map.
- Step 1: identify the user touchpoints. In this step, you are plotting the user journey—the interactions that users have with your library, resource, program, or service. Touchpoints can include online, service desk, appointment, in-person, etc. Once you have identified the touchpoints, plot them on the map chronologically.
- Step 2: identify opportunities for improvement. Are any steps in the user journey causing pain points, frustration, or friction? Are there any areas where users need help or clarification? This involves understanding what users want and need from their library and creating marketing materials that resonate with them.

- Step 3: create a visual representation of the customer journey. This step can be done using various tools like flowcharts, diagrams, or a storyboard. Include as much detail as possible in the visual representation so the library marketing team can understand the customer's experience. Including comments or notes to provide further context and insight is also helpful. Once the customer or user journey map has been created, it can be used to identify any potential pain points or issues that the customer may experience. The user or customer journey has five stages: awareness, consideration, conversion, retention, and advocacy.
    - Awareness. During this stage, the customer becomes aware of the library's services and offerings through advertising, word-of-mouth, or other forms of outreach. This critical stage requires library marketing professionals to focus on creating a strong, positive first impression.
    - Consideration. During this stage, the customer considers the library's services and decides whether to use the resources and services or attend the program. This is where library marketing professionals should focus on creating a strong value proposition and demonstrating the library's commitment to customer service.
    - Conversion. During this stage, the customer has decided to use the library's services, and the library marketing team should focus on delivering a positive customer experience. This could involve offering special outreach initiatives, helpful customer service, or incentives to encourage users to return.
    - Retention. At this stage, the library marketing team should focus on building customer loyalty and creating a strong connection with the customer. This could involve providing personalized customer service or sending follow-up emails to ensure customer satisfaction.
    - Advocacy. At this stage, the customer has become a strong advocate for the library's services and will likely recommend them to others. This is a great opportunity for library marketing professionals to capitalize on the customer's enthusiasm and create a powerful word-of-mouth marketing campaign.

User Journey Map Worksheet

		Awareness	Consideration	Conversion	Retention	Advocacy
Objectives	User's desired outcome and the steps they will take to achieve it.					
Needs	User's current needs and the actions they need to take to achieve them.					
Feelings	User's current and anticipated feelings throughout the customer journey.					
Barriers	Any obstacles that the user may encounter while trying to reach their desired outcome.					

Figure 15. The user journey map worksheet.

The user journey map worksheet provides a deep understanding of customer objectives, needs, feelings, and barriers to progress in alignment with each user or customer journey stage.

- The objectives section of the customer journey map worksheet should include the customer's desired outcome and the steps they will take to achieve it, including the desired duration of the journey. It should also include measures to track progress and ensure the customer's needs are met.
- The needs section should include the customer's current needs and the actions they need to take to achieve them.
- The feelings section should include the customer's current and anticipated feelings throughout the customer journey. This includes their current level of satisfaction, their views on their progress, and their expectations. It should also include the customer's anticipated feelings at each journey stage and the expected response.
- The barriers section should include any obstacles the customer may encounter while trying to reach their desired outcome. This includes physical, financial, or psychological barriers that may hinder progress. It should also include any external factors such as competition, regulations, or market conditions that may affect the customer's journey.

AFFINITY DIAGRAMMING

Another way to help you identify patterns and trends in the data is by using affinity diagramming. Affinity diagramming is a way to organize data into groups. To create an affinity diagram, write all the data points on sticky notes, then group similar ones. For example, suppose you are collecting data about user needs. In that case, you might group the data points into categories like "needs more information" or "needs an easier way to do X." After you have grouped the data points, you can start to identify patterns and trends. These patterns and trends will help you create a persona based on real data from your users.

USER PERSONAS

Personas are fictitious characters that represent a real segment of your users. They are based on data gathered from user research, such as interviews, surveys, and focus groups, and they embody your users' goals, needs, and frustrations. This data can come from user interviews, surveys, observations, and focus groups. Once you have this data, you can start to see patterns emerge. These patterns will help you identify your users' goals, needs, and frustrations; then, you can start to design solutions that address those needs. Understanding our users on an emotional level will also help build strong relationships with them.

Users who feel understood and valued are more likely to use and value your services. But what about users who don't fit into the persona you've created? What about users with disabilities, users from different cultures, or users with different needs? The answer is simple: create multiple personas. By creating multiple personas, you can address the needs of all your users. You don't need a separate persona for each user, but you should have enough variety to cover all your bases. Developing personas can help you answer important questions that you should be asking: Who are your users? To whom are we providing services? What are their personalities, motivations, key facts, and preferred communication channels? Do you have direct quotes from these users? Include them in your persona.

When developing personas, remember that they should be based on actual data you have collected. Do not make assumptions about your users; let the data guide you. Avoid stereotypes. Every user is an individual with unique needs and goals.

Once you have developed your personas, you can use them to guide your marketing decisions. When making changes to your resource or service, ask, does this benefit my user? If the answer is no, then the change is not worth making. By continuously keeping your users' needs in mind, you can ensure that your resource or service meets their needs and provides a positive experience.

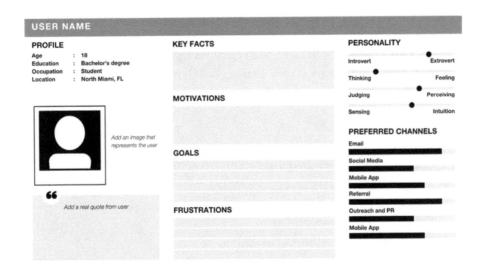

Figure 16. Create personas to help identify patterns in your customer base.

TESTING AND ITERATING LIBRARY MARKETING SOLUTIONS

Once libraries have developed a prototype, they need to test and iterate their library marketing solutions to ensure they are effective and engaging for their target audience. They can also use user testing to get direct feedback from their target audience and use analytics tools to track user behavior and identify areas for improvement.

Many methods are available to test marketing solutions, ranging from simple A/B testing to more complex approaches, such as the 8D approach for libraries or the Six Sigma process. Each solution provides a unique way to ensure marketing solutions are successfully tailored to its target audience. While these options provide a good start, there may be other easier or more effective methods depending on the project context. Ultimately, exploring all potential options for maximizing results when testing marketing solutions is important.

A/B Testing. A/B testing involves creating two versions of a resource, program, or service —version A and version B—and testing them against each other to determine which yields better results. For example, if a library marketer wanted to test two different versions of an email campaign targeting new memberships at a local public library branch office, they could use A/B testing techniques by sending out version A of their email campaign to half of their target audience while simultaneously sending out version B of their email campaign to the other half of their target audience and then measuring the response rate from both groups to see which version was more successful.

The 8D Approach. The 8D approach employs eight steps that focus on using data collection and analysis as well as team collaboration for problem identification, root cause analysis, and corrective action development:
- define
- describe
- discover (data collection)
- diagnose (root cause analysis)
- design (corrective action development)
- develop (implementation plan)
- deliver (results measurement)
- disposition (verification of results)

By following this approach, librarians can ensure they have considered all relevant factors before deciding on a solution.

The Six Sigma Process. The Six Sigma Process involves five steps (DMAIC):
- define
- measure
- analyze
- improve
- control

This framework helps organizations drive improvement by focusing on user requirements through data collection and analysis to address any potential issues or opportunities quickly and efficiently. By utilizing this process, libraries can focus on improving user satisfaction while simultaneously reducing costs associated with marketing efforts.

EXAMPLE EMPATHIC SURVEY QUESTIONS

- Triggers of use. What made you use the library today?
- What was your experience with using the library?
- User customization. How do you reinvent your use of the library?
- What are some intangible attributes of the library? How do you use the library?
- Unarticulated user needs. Are there any areas that you always need help with?
- Here are four questions that can help you gain insights into your users' emotions and needs:
  - What are the user's unspoken needs?

- How does the user feel in this environment?
- What are the user's values?
- How can we put the user first?
- Here is a second set of preliminary things that you should know that can help you consider how to market the library to your communities with empathy:
    - What is the library's mission?
    - How does the library serve its community?
    - Who is your target audience?
    - What needs does your target audience have that the library can address?
    - What are the unique selling points (USP) of the library?
    - How can we communicate the value of the library to our community?

See also Appendix C for more marketing plan information.

APPENDIX B: THE FIRST VALUES FRAMEWORK FOR LIBRARY MARKETING QUESTIONS

As covered in Chapter 9, the FIRST values framework (fellow-feeling, identification, responsiveness, self-awareness, thoughtfulness) is designed to

- enable a collaborative planning process to help your team understand the unspoken needs of your users and stakeholders;
- push you to focus on the users of your library and their needs as opposed to solving problems that are not relevant to the mission of the library and the larger institution;
- help you understand that marketing with empathy and innovation requires a focus on your target audiences and their needs, not just on identity and branding alone; and
- help develop and define a shared understanding and group identity.

Here are some questions to consider when developing your FIRST values framework:

Fellow-feeling—the ability to understand and share another person's feelings. To apply this value to your design process, ask yourself questions such as:
- What are my users feeling?
- What might they be feeling in the future?
- How can I design for their feelings?

Identification—the ability to see yourself in others. Ask:
- How can I identify with my users?
- What do we have in common?
- What do they need from the library?
- What purpose does the library serve for them?
- How does it fit into their lives?
- Do they visit for leisure activities like browsing books or attending events?

Responsiveness—the ability to respond appropriately to another person's needs and feelings. Ask:
- What does my user need from me right now?
- How can I show them that I understand their needs?
- What kind of response will be most helpful?

- How can I provide timely responses to inquiries or feedback from patrons and be proactive in addressing issues, such as insufficient resources or outdated technology before patrons bring them to attention themselves?
- How can prompt communication show users that their concerns are taken seriously and foster goodwill between library professionals and patrons?

Self-awareness—the ability to understand your own emotions and how they affect your interactions with users. Ask:
- Am I feeling empathy for my users? Or am I feeling something else?
- What might be getting in the way of my empathy?
- How can I manage my own emotions so that they don't interfere with my work?
- How can I practice self-awareness when performing marketing activities to monitor any changes in the user base or new trends within the industry more effectively?
- Should I keep up with industry news through publications like *Library Journal, which provide valuable information on current topics such as budget cuts or book trends while also serving as inspiration for future campaigns?*

Thoughtfulness—the ability to think about what you say and do before you act. Ask:
- Is this solution thoughtful?
- What could I do to make it more thoughtful?
- How can I treat users with compassion during all interactions, whether face-to-face at a reference desk or through digital platforms such as social media accounts or web pages?
- How can I show appreciation when someone is interested in what the library has to offer (such as attending an event) but also provide personalized service when possible (like recognizing repeat visitors)?
- How will these solutions impact my users?
- What are the potential risks of these solutions?

By following this process, you will not only be able to come up with more empathic solutions but also better understand your users and their needs.

APPENDIX C: MARKETING PLAN

Developing a successful marketing plan based on empathy requires a thorough understanding of the library's mission, vision, core values, target audiences, user personas, and the current situation.

- Analyze the library's strengths, weaknesses, opportunities, and threats (S.W.O.T. analysis) to develop effective marketing and outreach strategies and tactics.
- Defining the objectives, costs, and evaluation plans for each strategy.
- Create a brand identity with key messages that represent the library.
- Consider ideas that could be implemented in the future.
- Assign roles and responsibilities to those involved in the campaign.
- Create an action plan schedule and budget for the marketing plan.
- Assess the marketing plan's success using indicators such as results and assessments.

Vision

When creating a library marketing plan, it is essential to include a clear vision. This vision should include the library's mission, values, purpose, and goals. Additionally, it should communicate what the library seeks to accomplish and how it plans to achieve its goals. With a solid and clear vision, the library can ensure that all marketing efforts are focused and targeted to reach the desired outcome.

Core Values

Consider core values that will guide the plan. Core values provide the foundation for your library's mission and purpose. Here are some examples of core values:

- Accessibility—ensuring that library services, materials, and programs are accessible to all members of the community
- Inclusion—embracing diversity, equity, and inclusion in library services and programs
- Education—providing educational opportunities for community members of all ages and backgrounds
- Innovation—exploring new technologies and services to provide the best experience for library users
- Collaboration—working together with other cultural institutions and community partners to promote the library's mission
- Accountability—being transparent and responsible for the library's actions and decisions.

- Stewardship—taking responsibility for the library's resources and infrastructure.

Executive Summary

The executive summary of a library marketing plan should do the following:
- Provide an overview of the library's marketing objectives and strategies
- Include information on the library's target audience, its services or resources, and what makes the library unique
- Discuss the library's goals for its marketing efforts, the methods it will use to reach potential customers, and the expected outcomes of its marketing plan.
- Include an overview of the budget and timeline for the marketing plan.

Target Audiences

When creating a library marketing plan, there are several target audiences to consider:
- Consider your target audience. Who are the people who are most likely to benefit from the services your library offers? Consider their age, gender, education level, interests, and any other demographics that may be relevant.
- Create user personas that represent groups of library users. This will help you visualize who your library is targeting and tailor your marketing plan accordingly.
- Empathy maps and user journey maps can be valuable tools to help you understand your target audience better. Empathy maps allow you to map out how your target audience may think, feel, say, and do, while user journey maps can help you understand the steps that a customer takes before, during, and after using your library services.

Situation Analysis

A library marketing plan should start with a situation analysis that includes
- A SWOT analysis is a great tool to assess a library's strengths, weaknesses, opportunities, and threats. It can help identify what the library does well and needs to improve on, as well as the potential opportunities and threats in the external environment.
- A needs assessment can help identify the needs of the library's target audience and the best way to reach them.

Marketing and Outreach Strategies and Tactics (or Objectives)

When creating a library marketing plan, there are a variety of marketing and outreach strategies and tactics that can be employed. Some of these include

- developing a website or social media presence to reach a broad audience,
- utilizing email campaigns to target specific patron groups,
- creating promotional materials to highlight library services,
- hosting events and workshops to engage the community and
- partnering with other departments, local businesses, or organizations to increase visibility.

When creating library marketing strategies:

- Consider your core values, asking what message you want to send, what principles you want to promote, and how your library can best serve its community.
- Consider how your library can provide unique services and resources that help to further your mission statement and reflect your core values.
- Create marketing campaigns that are tailored to your library's goals and that help to get the word out about the services and resources your library offers.
- Develop an effective marketing strategy to inform users of upcoming events, programs, services, and resources.

Every library is unique, so it is vital to consider the individual goals and audience of the library when determining which marketing and outreach strategies and tactics to include in the plan. Here is an example of how to present your strategies in your marketing plan:

- strategies
- tactics
- cost
- evaluation—indicators of success

Brand Identity

A great brand identity section of a marketing plan should

- Include a detailed description of the company's brand, including its mission and values, logo and tagline, target audience, positioning statement, key messages, and any other vital components that make up the brand and
- offer insight into how the library plans to use its brand identity to differentiate itself from competitors and build loyalty.

Key Messages

To create your marketing plan section, use compelling and effective key messages that will help you reach your goals:
- Focus on the key messages you want to communicate to your target audience.
- Make sure they are concise, clear, and compelling.
- Messages should reflect the goals and objectives of your organization as well as the values and mission of your brand.
- Make sure to tailor your messages to the needs and interests of your target audience.

Campaign/Action Plan Schedule/Timeline

Creating a schedule/timeline for your library marketing plan is a crucial step in ensuring your campaign is successful. Here are some tips that can help you get started:
- Establish your goals. Before you begin creating your timeline, establish the goals of your campaign. What do you want to achieve? What are the objectives (tactics)?
- Identify the tasks that need to be completed to achieve those goals.
- Assign dates to each task so that you can better track progress and ensure that the project is completed on time.
- Set checkpoints throughout the timeline to ensure that tasks are completed on time, and the project is on track.
- Monitor your progress and adjust as needed to ensure that the timeline is followed, and the goals are met.

Budget

You may have a budget for special programs and events that can be utilized for marketing purposes. Creating a budget section can be a great way to stay on track and ensure all your marketing efforts are cost-effective and have a great ROI.

Communication Samples and Prototypes

Add your communication samples and prototypes for your campaign and focus on creating both digital and traditional communication samples, as this will help reach a greater audience while keeping with the library's brand. Digital communications include
- social media posts, emails, website content, and

- traditional communications include newspaper ads, flyers, and radio or television advertisements.

Use these samples and prototypes to test your campaigns and plans and to ensure effectiveness with your users.

Assessment Results/Reporting/Evaluation/Indicators of Success

- A successful library marketing plan should include indicators of success such as increased website traffic, increased number of patrons, increased circulation of library materials, and higher attendance at library events.
- Assessments should be conducted to measure the effectiveness of different marketing strategies and materials, such as surveys of patrons or tracking the number of views and shares of library-related posts on social media.
- By tracking these indicators, library professionals can gain insight into which strategies are working and which need to be adjusted.

Media List

- Adding a media list to your marketing plan entails compiling a list of organizations, departments, websites, newspapers, radio, and TV stations that you can connect with to help promote your library and its events.
- The list should include contact information such as names and contact information (email, social media handles, etc.).
- Once you have compiled the list, use it to send out press releases, media alerts, and invitations.
- Regularly update the list with new contacts and keep track of responses from contacts in another document.

Glossary

A/B testing. A method of experimentation in which two versions of a web page are shown to users randomly and statistical analysis is used to determine which version performs better.

Accessibility. The quality or state of being accessible; the quality or state of being easy to approach, enter, or use.

Action plan or plan of action. A detailed plan outlining actions that need to be taken to achieve a specific goal. It is typically composed of steps or activities that will help achieve the desired outcome. Action plans can be used for short and long-term goals and may include deadlines, resources needed, and people responsible for each step. A plan of action should be detailed, realistic, and achievable.

Brainstorming. Brainstorming is a technique used to generate new ideas or solutions. A group usually engages in this technique, which involves quickly coming up with as many ideas as possible.

Brand. A brand is a name, term, design, symbol, or something else that makes a company or product stand out from its competitors in the eyes of the user. This makes the user loyal to the company or product.

Brand awareness. The level of consumer recognition of a brand. How well do consumers know a brand and its products or services?

Branding. The term "branding" has many definitions, but at its core, "branding" is creating a unique product, service, or company identity. This identity can be a name, logo, slogan, or other visual elements. Branding means making your resource or service stand out and giving it a clear, easy-to-recognize name (see library branding).

Churn. Used to describe when a customer or user stops using a resource, program, or service.

Collateral materials. Any materials that are used to support or promote a resource, program, or service. This can include brochures, flyers, posters, social media posts, email marketing campaigns, and even website content.

Communication plan. A written document that outlines how an organization will communicate with its audiences. The plan should include the organization's goals and objectives, who will be responsible for various tasks, and what communication channels will be used.

Communication. Refers to any means of reaching out to potential and existing users through social media channels.

Confirmation bias. The tendency to search for, interpret, favor, and recall information in a way that confirms one's preexisting beliefs or hypotheses.

Conversion. When someone takes an action, you want them to take, such as borrowing a book or signing up for a library program.

Conversion tracking. Conversion tracking is a method of tracking the effectiveness of an online marketing campaign or advertisement. It helps track the number of people who complete a desired action after seeing an advertisement or engaging with a marketing campaign. This action could be signing up for a newsletter or downloading a resource. Conversion tracking helps businesses measure the success and return on investment of campaigns and advertisements.

Cost-benefit analysis. Cost-benefit analysis is a process used to determine the potential costs and benefits associated with a proposed project or policy. It involves quantifying the expected costs and benefits of a decision and then comparing them to determine the overall value. Cost-benefit analysis is often used to help inform decision-making in business, government, and other organizations.

Diversity. The presence of people who are different in a group or organization. The state or quality of being diverse; variety.

Empathic design. A human-centered approach in which designers seek to understand their users' needs, wants, and values. This can be done through user research such as interviews, surveys, and user testing. Empathic design creates resources, services, programs, and experiences that meet users' needs, not just what the designer thinks is best.

Empathic marketing. Used to describe a marketing approach focusing on understanding and catering to customer needs. This approach is based on the idea that if a company can understand the user's needs and desires, it can create resources, services, and experiences that appeal to users.

Empathic library marketing. A method of marketing that focuses on understanding and addressing the emotional needs of library users. It is an approach that puts the user at the center of the marketing strategy and seeks to understand their needs, motivations, and feelings. This type of marketing focuses on building relationships with users and fostering a sense of community.

Empathy map. Used by researchers and designers to gain a deeper understanding of their users. It is a way to visualize and document user needs, wants, and values.

Empathy. The ability to understand and share another person's feelings.

Engagement. Efforts to engage potential and existing library users through various activities, including programs, promotions, collections, events, etc.

Equity. The realization that all must be treated according to the same standards and provided equitable opportunities.

Human-centered design. Human-centered design is a process for creating products, services, and environments based on the needs and preferences of the people using them. This method puts the user first instead of the designer. Because of this, products, resources, services, experiences, and environments are more empathetic, easy to use, and effective.

Ideation (verb: ideate). Ideation is the process of developing or brainstorming new ideas or solutions or generating new ideas.

Inclusion. Recognizing the diversity in each person and building a community around diverse experiences.

Iterative prototyping. A process of creating and refining a prototype of a project or product. It involves creating a prototype, testing it, making changes based on the testing results, and then testing the prototype again.

Key performance indicators (KPIs). Companies, organizations, and institutions like libraries use precise figures to measure how well they're doing and how close they are to reaching their goals. KPIs are different for each industry, set of goals, and part of the performance being measured.

Library branding. Creating and using an organization's unique name, logo, and identity. This branding can promote the library and its services to the community. Library branding helps potential and current users recognize your library from all the others and feel a sense of connection to it. Branding can increase pride in your library and its services while helping people remember what it offers.

Library marketing. Promoting awareness of the library and its resources through promotion can be done through various methods, such as social media, print materials, events, and more. Library marketing aims to reach potential users and get them excited about the library's resources, programs, and services.

Library outreach. A program that enables the staff to go into the community and offer library services to people who might not otherwise have access, such as bringing library services to underserved populations in urban areas or providing mobile library services to rural areas. Providing library resources and services to people who are unable to visit the library in person is known as library outreach. This is another form of community engagement. This can involve providing library resources and services to senior citizens, people with disabilities, the homebound, and those who reside in rural areas. Library professionals could also use outreach tabling (see definition) to promote the library and its resources by attending schools and community groups.

Library swag. Refers to the promotional items that a library gives, such as t-shirts, pens, or tote bags during outreach events, tabling, and events.

Market research. Gathering information about customers, competitors, and the market, in general, to help make better decisions.

Market segmentation. The process of dividing a market into different customer groups with similar needs or wants.

Marketing campaign. A plan or strategy designed to achieve specific marketing objectives.

Marketing plan. A company's marketing activities are mapped out in a plan. It details the company's marketing goals and strategies and provides a timeline for when those activities will take place. A marketing plan is a detailed roadmap that outlines the steps a company will take to achieve its marketing goals. The plan should include a SWOT analysis, objectives, strategies, tactics, a budget, and an evaluation strategy.

Needs assessment. A needs assessment is a tool used to determine what needs or wants are currently unmet by a group or individual or can help identify areas where an organization can improve.

Needs-based approach. A method of identifying and addressing the needs of individuals or groups. This approach focuses on understanding the individual or group's needs and then developing a plan to address those needs.

Outreach plan. An outreach plan is a plan of action designed to increase a target audience's visibility and engagement with a product, service, cause, or organization.

Outreach tabling. A type of marketing activity where an organization sets up a table at a public event or place to promote their cause, showcase their resources, or recruit new members. Outreach tabling for libraries is setting up tables in public places to advertise and promote library services. This usually means setting up a table with materials and people who can talk to people and answer questions about library services. It can also include giving people demos and hands-on activities to show them what the library offers.

Pain point. A problem or challenge that a customer or client faces. It is typically something that causes them frustration, annoyance, or difficulty.

Persona. Fictional characters are created to represent different segments of a target market. Personas help marketers better understand their target customers' needs and wants and develop marketing strategies that are more likely to resonate with them.

PESTLE analysis. A framework used to analyze the macroenvironmental factors that may affect the operations of a business. PESTLE stands for political, economic, social, technological, legal, and environmental factors. It is used to assess these factors' current and potential impact on a company's success.

Positioning statement. An internal strategic statement used to guide the overall brand or product strategy.

Product. In libraries, the term "product" may refer to physical items that users can borrow, such as books, scores, DVDs, CDs, etc. It can also encompass digital products, such as e-books and audiobooks, which patrons can access online. In library marketing, "product" can refer to programs, resources, or services that are offered to the community.

Program. In libraries, it typically refers to organized events, outreach, activities, or workshops designed to engage and educate the community. Library programs can include book clubs, author talks, children's storytimes, educational workshops, and more.

Promotion. Refers to efforts to publicize the library's presence and offerings in various ways.

Prototype development (library marketing). Prototyping for library marketing is creating a representation of a library's marketing campaign or strategy to test or show how it will work in practice. This can include creating mockups of websites, designing marketing materials, or creating visuals to show how the library's services or resources can be used. Prototyping for library marketing can also involve creating user scenarios.

Prototype development (product or system design). A way of quickly creating a working model of a product or system. It is used to test and refine ideas before making a final version. It can help designers understand user needs and identify problems with a design before investing time and resources into a final product.

Resource. A broad term that can encompass both physical and digital materials available to users, it includes books, databases, magazines, and other sources of information that users can access for research and learning.

Resource/program/service Nirvana. A term used to describe the perfect combination of marketing resources, programs, and services that meet all of the needs of a particular customer or organization. It represents a state of total satisfaction and completion.

Return on investment (marketing). The return on investment (ROI) in marketing measures the profitability of a marketing campaign or activity. It is calculated by dividing the marketing activity's net profit by the total amount of money invested. The resulting percentage is the return on investment.

Service. In libraries, it refers to the assistance and support librarians and library professionals provide patrons. This includes reference and research services, computer and internet access, meeting room reservations, and other services that enhance the library experience.

Strategic marketing plan. A strategic marketing plan is a document that outlines a company's overall marketing strategy. It includes objectives, tactics, and strategies for reaching the company's target market. The plan outlines the organization's marketing objectives and how they will be achieved and measured. It also includes information on the organization's target markets, positioning, and brand strategy. It is usually prepared by a company's marketing team in collaboration with other departments.

SWOT analysis. A strategic planning tool evaluates a business or project's strengths, weaknesses, opportunities, and threats. Strengths and weaknesses are internal, while opportunities and threats are external.

Target audience. A specific group of people within the general public who are identified as the desired recipients of a particular message or campaign.

Touchpoint. A touchpoint is where customers and clients contact a company or brand. This can be physical or digital, including everything from a library's website to its physical location and social media accounts.

Usability test. A test determines how easy or difficult it is for users to use a particular software application or website.

User engagement. The level of interaction and involvement that a user has with a product, service, or brand.

User experience design. The process of making products that give users meaningful and valuable experiences. This is the design of the whole experience of using a product (resources), including the interface, the interactions, the visual design, and the user journey.

User experience. How a person feels when interacting with a company, its products, or its services. It includes everything from how a person discovers a company or product to how they interact with it to how they feel after using it.

User (customer) journey map. A path a user takes to complete a task or set of goals on a website or app. It is also known as a customer journey or buyer's journey. It is usually shown as a flowchart that shows the steps a user must take to finish the task.

Value proposition. A concise statement that highlights the unique benefits and value of a product, service, or solution to its target audience, explaining why a user should choose it over alternatives and addressing their needs or problems.

About the Author

Sabine Jean Dantus, an outreach and reference librarian at Florida International University Libraries in Miami, Florida, takes immense pride in her Haitian-American heritage. Sabine has a B.S. in communication from Florida International University. She also has an M.S. in mass media and journalism and a M.S. in library science from Pennsylvania Western University Clarion. Her expertise and interest lie in empathy-based marketing, outreach, user experience, instruction, and library communication. Sabine is completing her doctoral degree in instructional technology and distance education. She is researching enhancing communication between librarians and first-generation college students in online, hybrid, and in-person learning settings. Sabine shares her thoughts on empathy, marketing, outreach, books, instruction, librarianship, and her doctoral journey on empathiclibrarian.com.